The
Warrior's
Meditation

Other books by Richard L. Haight

The Unbound Soul

Inspirience: Meditation Unbound

The Psychedelic Path

The
Warrior's
Meditation

Richard L. Haight

Shinkaikan Body, Mind, Spirit LLC

www.richardlhaight.com

ISBN 978-0999210093
Library of Congress Control Number:2019919963

Disclaimer:

1. Some names and identifying details have been changed to protect the privacy of individuals.

2. This book is not intended as a substitute for the medical or psychological advice of physicians or psychiatrists. The reader should regularly consult health practitioner in matters relating to his or her physical or mental/emotional health and particularly with respect to any symptoms that may require diagnosis or medical attention.

Published by Shinkaikan Body, Mind, Spirit LLC

www.richardlhaight.com

Table of Contents

Acknowledgments

First, I would like to thank my martial arts instructor, Shizen Osaki, for assisting and supporting my meditation explorations. Without his assistance, I am sure this fresh approach to meditation and awareness could not have come to fruition.

Second, I give my sincere appreciation to my student, Kris Kokay, who inspired me to write this book. To my students Linda LaTores and Barbara Becker, I give my thanks for their extremely helpful feedback on the manuscript.

I would also like to thank my other students for their dedication to the meditative process and their many questions, which have served to clarify the content of this book.

To my copy-editors, Edward Austin Hall and Hester Lee Furey (who also proofread), I extend my most sincere appreciation for helping me to find my voice! My cover designer Nathaniel Dasco, I thank for the stunning cover design.

My wife, Teruko Haight, has provided patience, support, and dedication to challenging my awareness in everyday life, an invaluable practice for which I am eternally grateful.

Finally, I offer gratitude to the many supporters who financially contributed to help pay for the publishing of this book. Please know that I couldn't have done this without your support.

Below, I list each contributor by name:

Barbara Becker
Linda LaTores
Neal Jepson
Dan Smith
Rona Bennett
Toni Hollenbeck
Kiri Varatharajan
Micheal Elliott
Gagandeep Singh
Scott Hughes
Jeffry Meyer
Irina Pushkina
John Bishop
Diane Wright
Spencer Udelson
Joop Tjeertes
Masaya Higuma
Roi Gary

From the depths of my heart, I thank you all!

Total Embodiment Methodology

Preface

As of the publishing of this book, I have been a dedicated meditator for more than 30 years, and I have been teaching meditation for more than a decade. From the start of my meditating practice as a teenager, I approached meditation solely as a spiritual tool. But last year, while discussing this book's development in a meditation class, one of my longtime students, Kris, suggested that I take a nonspiritual approach with the book, to make the Total Embodiment Methodology available to more people.

Kris reasoned that our approach to meditation is entirely principle-based, so the practice could benefit anyone of any background, even people who are not interested in spiritual awakening. As I had always used meditation for the purpose of spiritual awakening, I had never considered making it available to the general public.

Although many people who practice TEM meditation report, as a result, experiencing a "spiritual" sense of connectedness with the universe, there is no reason that the Total Embodiment Method could not enhance anyone's life. After all, the desire for life-enrichment is common to all human beings.

Of all the life-enrichment options available to us, meditation may be one of the wisest choices, for it leads to lasting beneficial changes in the brain that positively affect our perception of every experience that we have thereafter.

Thanks to personality, interests, and backgrounds coming into the practice, certain people may interpret the inner transformation that comes of a powerful meditation practice as being spiritual, whereas others might not think of it in spiritual terms at all. I'm not sure the jargon used to describe our inner transformation matters so much as does the transformation itself — the enrichment of our lives. In the final analysis, if people are becoming more aware, more loving, and more capable as a result of their meditation practice, then who is to argue?

With Kris' suggestion in mind, this book is written to be of service to anyone who seeks life enrichment through greater awareness. Regardless of your background or beliefs, the principles of meditation conveyed through this book, if practiced, will prove tangibly beneficial to your life.

With sustained practice, I am confident that the awareness and inner clarity you will gain from practicing the meditations herein will help you to be a better teacher, student, parent, child, spouse, friend, employer, or employee, for no matter your position, you will be a more integrated, more capable individual than you would be otherwise. So long as your aim is to live a healthier, more vibrant, clear, inspired, authentic existence, the practices within this book can be of service to you.

Finally, it is my deepest hope that the meditative experiences you have will help you to see the beauty that is within you — and all around you.

Introduction

When I first began martial arts training in Japan with my teacher Shizen Osaki, I was surprised to find that he allocated only a few seconds before and after each training session for meditation. I have practiced under many instructors during my life of martial arts training. Some of those instructors employ meditation at the start and end of every training session, whereas others do not. Of the teachers who employ meditation, none of them ever meditated for just a few seconds, which seemed an impossibly short time to reach a meditative state. Although I was already a lifelong meditator, even before joining Osaki Sensei's dojo, the two-second meditation ritual defied my abilities.

For many years, I went through the motions of the two-second meditations without asking about it. No one else asked about it either, so I assumed it was just a ritual with no practical meaning. Personally, I never once reached a notable state of meditation during the many thousands of times that I experienced those two-second meditations.

Eventually, I attained a senior level and began training privately with my teacher. During one private training session I asked about the ritual. My teacher paused for a moment before he answered (in Japanese, as were all of our conversations).

> That is an excellent question. In traditional Japanese martial arts, we do not use the teaching models found in primary schools. School learning is passive. There, students expect the teacher to give them everything.
>
> I feel that long-term exposure to passive learning makes students less mentally sharp. For martial arts training, students' minds must be sharp, so I feel the school teaching model is insufficient for our purposes. In our martial arts training, students are expected to do research on their own, beyond what I show them, to discover the inner secrets.
>
> Although it may seem as if our approach to learning is very difficult, I feel people develop more from doing their own research and exploration than they do when they are just told how to do everything, which engenders a lazy mindset. I feel that doing your own research brings out your innate intelligence, and that makes you a much more powerful martial artist and human being.
>
> With the idea of research in mind, I think your meditation question provides a great opportunity for exploration. I am eager to hear what you discover.

After thinking about it for several weeks, it occurred to me that the lifestyle and duties of the Samurai necessitated a very different approach to meditation than what monks typically practiced.

The Samurai required instant access to profound inner silence under the tremendous chaos and pressure of battlefield combat against other highly trained warriors. Sitting with eyes closed for hours on end would not allow a warrior to fulfill his duties, nor would it lead to the instant calm awareness that he required when attacked unexpectedly or chaotically — a possibility about which a warrior must always be mindful. A warrior's practice had to be simple and effective, period.

Of course, many ancient arts decay with time and lack of need and, thus, become fluff-filled, formalized traditions absent their original practicality — mere shells of their former glory. That said, within those traditions, if we look, we can still find hints of lost mindsets. The two-second meditation is an example of just such a hint.

Although the arts that Osaki Sensei taught were still highly effective, surely some decay had occurred over the centuries. To maintain the viability of any structure, each generation must view it with fresh eyes to revitalize it. I could not be sure that my answer to the two-second meditation riddle was correct, but it made sense, and it provided a powerful challenge to my meditation capabilities. I was eager to begin my research.

Once I felt certain about the value of my answer, I discussed it with my teacher, who listened intently and then paused for a time to consider before he replied.

> I believe you have found the right answer. Now you must discover a way of meditation that puts you into an instant, calm clarity, from which you can move properly, without thought, under extreme martial pressure. Please keep in mind that two seconds may be only a hint of what is required. Against a skilled opponent, even two seconds is too long. I am eager to hear what you discover.

Shortly after this conversation, I had a visionary experience that gave me a powerful hint for my training. I saw that we would need to combine our martial arts practice with the Japanese therapy art of sotai-ho that I was licensed to practice.

I saw that by combining the two arts, a profound awareness would emerge that would transform both arts and reveal the meditation method I sought. Although I feared Sensei would think I was insane for having a "vision," at the next private training session, I told Sensei what I was shown.

Osaki Sensei told me that Kamiizumi Ise no Kami, the founder of our sword art, is said to have had a vision which guided him in the creation of his martial system, Shinkage-ryu. Shinkage-ryu, unlike other arts of the day, was meant to preserve the life of the enemy.

Kamiizumi Sensei felt it was a shame to kill an enemy unnecessarily, for he understood the quality of person it took to be Samurai. Kamiizumi Sensei felt that each warrior was a vital contributor to society, and so, preserving each life, where possible, was the best strategy for society.

Thanks to the vision of Kamiizumi Ise no Kami and the superior effectiveness of his martial system, Shinkage-ryu was chosen by the Shogun (then the supreme military leader of Japan) to be his official sword art. Shinkage-ryu remained the official art of the Shogun for the next 400 years, until the fall of the Japanese feudal system. Because of its incredible efficiency and its vision for a positive society, Shinkage-ryu is the most revered elite Samurai art in Japanese history.

As Osaki Sensei spoke to me about Kamiizumi Sensei's vision, he was visibly inspired. Osaki Sensei reminded me that I had performed sotai-ho on his painful knee once, and the knee obviously improved as a result. He said he was eager to learn my therapy method and see what might come of combining therapy and martial arts training. He suggested that we set aside several hours each day for our collaboration.

We continued our daily, private training for several years, and as we refined our understanding of the arts, we began to find ourselves in profoundly meditated states, almost effortlessly. Fundamentally, the method that we used for our meditation was pure feeling, intention, and relaxed awareness — the result of dedicated, daily, long-term, awareness training under intense physical and psychological pressure.

As I neared the end of my training, having already received Masters Licenses in the four Samurai arts that Osaki Sensei taught, I wondered how I could convey our meditation method to others, for teaching was now my responsibility. I didn't think what we were doing could work for anyone who was not already highly trained.

I discussed the issue with Osaki Sensei. We agreed that the meditation had profoundly affected our lives in every way, and that we were much better people because of it. We agreed that it would greatly benefit society if it were made available to the general public.

Sensei said he was eager for me to find a way to pass the meditation on to beginners. I lamented that I lacked a step-by-step method that would quickly lead beginners to the depth of awareness we were accessing. Sensei then asked me what type of meditation I practiced before coming to his dojo.

I explained that I'd never had formal meditation training, but that I had been a daily meditator since the age of sixteen. I started with a basic meditation that I learned from my girlfriend. As I was a dedicated martial arts student from age twelve, I was eager to find a way to meditate while I practiced, so I began gradually modifying the meditation approach that I had learned from my girlfriend. By the time I joined Osaki Sensei's dojo, my approach was entirely different from the meditation that I began with as a teen.

As a result of my practice before joining Osaki Sensei's dojo, I could already walk, talk, and do many other activities while meditated, but I could not get into the meditated state instantly, nor could I use it under the intensity of my teacher's attacks.

Sensei asked me to share my former method with him. After experiencing it, he said he was certain that it could be easily modified to create a step-by-step system that leads into the functional, instant awareness that we were experiencing. I retired from my job and dedicated my remaining time in Japan to intensive training with Sensei. We practiced together six hours a day, every day except during weekends, for the remainder of my stay in Japan. We made rapid progress in the arts that we practiced, and we refined our teaching modality.

In this book, I will share the basic TEM method, which is an approach unlike any meditation that you are likely to have heard of. After conveying the basics, we will explore how to blend meditation into your daily life, so that you are no longer held back by the requirements of a quiet space, specific body postures, and dogmas.

You may be surprised by just how simple and effective the method is. Within just a few sessions, you will be able to meditate with relative ease, even with your eyes open. And with a little more practice, you'll be able to walk, drive, and accomplish many other activities during meditation.

Through short, daily meditation sessions, the incredible benefits of meditation will open up to you through your active, daily life. Eventually, you will fully embody meditation, as a way of being, not just a doing. I call this way of being total embodiment.

Throughout the process of your meditation journey, you will be priming your mind and body for greater health and capabilities. Your brain will become more elastic, and you will experience more calm clarity and inspiration.

Surprisingly, there is much scientific research into the health benefits associated with regular meditation practice. To summarize that research, meditation boosts health through improved immune function, and through decreased cellular inflammation and pain. Meditation boosts happiness by increasing positive emotion while decreasing anxiety, depression, and stress.

Of course, meditation improves your ability to introspect, which provides a more holistic, grounded life perspective. Regular meditation can also improve your social life as it increases emotional intelligence and compassion while reducing feelings of insecurity.

You may be surprised to discover that regular meditation practice positively improves your brain by increasing gray matter. Specifically, cortical thickness increases in areas related to paying attention. Brain volume also increases in areas related to positive emotions, emotional regulation, and self-control. These vital changes increase psychological well-being while reducing emotional reactivity.

According to *Psychology Today*, the research shows that you may also notice improvements in memory, creativity, and abstract thinking (Seppala).

Although these benefits are amazing, being honest, it takes a lot of time and effort to realize these benefits; and most of us just don't have the time or energy to put into a formal, daily meditation practice, so we don't get the benefits ....

So that brings us back to the differences between the Total Embodiment Method and other forms of meditation. TEM will get you those benefits faster and easier, and take you to a deeper place than you might imagine, with your eyes open and while blending with your active daily life.

No longer does meditation need to be a retreat from life, for you will be able to digest what life throws at you as you experience it. No longer will you be building up undigested emotions and frustrations, for life itself will be a cleansing and correcting process that will effectively reveal the truest you.

In my opinion, TEM is the best-kept secret in self-improvement, cognitive enhancement, and stress relief in the world. I have little doubt that this type of dynamic meditation was known to the elite Samurai, for it is hinted at in the two-second meditation ritual.

Although I doubt the method was ever formally taught as a modality, those who were truly dedicated to training could discover it during advanced training. Through this book, the highly flexible, highly effective method is codified and made accessible to the general public.

With some dedication to daily practice, you will be able to meditate while walking and talking, and even while working!

Imagine having all of the scientifically proven benefits of long-term, daily meditation available to you without having to retreat from life to enter a state of meditation (although that may be in order from time to time).

Eventually, with regular TEM practice, the transformative power of meditation will be available to you any time you want, with a mere flash of intention.

The genius of the Samurai was efficiency. They were not interested in sedentary meditation as an adjunct to martial arts training (though many Samurai surely did sedentary meditation as a religious practice), because that approach would be useless on the battlefield, where calm, clear, vibrant awareness was needed in an instant, in the face of gruesome injury and imminent death.

With efficiency in mind, we will carefully differentiate meditation methods that are born of religious practice from ones that emerge from a need for practical application, for such discernment can save you a lot of time and effort if you are not primarily interested in religious practice.

Although the meditations that I teach can certainly lead to tremendous spiritual awakenings, as is attested by many a student of mine, at base they are warrior ways. To acknowledge the origins of TEM, I call the first and most basic meditation the Warrior's Meditation.

With regular practice, through daily life, you can effortlessly meditate in just minutes, seconds, or even instantly, depending on how acclimated your brain is to the meditation. It truly is amazing.

In the process of your meditation journey, you will also notice that dysfunctional thoughts, feelings, and behaviors begin to dissolve from your life, to be replaced by a sense of inner peace and fulfillment. You will begin to experience flow states that empower success in everything that you set your mind to, including your relationships and your vocation. You will experience more inspiration and creativity, and you will learn more efficiently and have better memory than you would otherwise. Your brain will begin to naturally release chemicals that will improve your health and vitality beyond where it would be if you didn't practice meditation daily. You will experience less stress, anxiety, and you may even begin to feel as if you are never alone, even when no one else is around. You will be more relaxed as old, unresolved mental and emotional issues fade away.

Moreover, you will eat, sleep, and live more completely than you thought possible. With persistent practice, you will be living an engaged life of vibrant awareness and connectivity, and that means you will be a wiser, more aware, more capable individual than you ever imagined.

Yes, you really can meditate like a Samurai master. And, what's more, you can do it with your eyes open, while talking, while walking, and eventually, even while working.

Not only will you learn, step-by-step, the approach that I discovered and refined in Japan under the tutelage of my martial arts teacher, Shizen Osaki, but along with this book, I am offering you a free 30-day trial of my daily online guided meditation class, which means that I will personally walk you through the steps of the Warrior's Meditation each day. You will find the link at the end of the book.

The aim, at least for my part, is that you be able to walk, talk, and work in vibrant awareness. And beyond that, it is my intention that vibrant clarity will be your lived reality. But regardless of whether you choose to avail yourself of the daily training opportunity with me, this book is going to open your eyes to possibilities that you've never imagined.

What will happen is this: each day, as you practice the short meditation, your brain will shift from the habitual, focused, stressful, agitated beta wave state that you have lived with by default all of your life, into the meditated flow state of alpha wave.

As you relax into a more expansive awareness, your brain will move beyond alpha and into theta, delta, and possibly even gamma-wave states that stimulate profoundly positive, lasting structural changes in your brain.

Not only will you be meditating here and there through your daily life, it will be easy and fun! What's more, you will not have to sit in uncomfortable positions for long periods, with your eyes closed, though you certainly can if you want.

With continued practice, you will be able to shift into deep states of awareness and clarity with a mere flash of intention. Imagine going to a job interview, and just before you meet your potential boss, you flash into a vibrant, calm, clarity that brings out your very best inner aspects. With the virtues of awareness, you are more likely to get that job, if it is a fit for you, than you would be otherwise.

With practice, you can rapidly reach deeper states of meditation than you could previously achieve, even with many years of sedentary meditation practice.

Why is that?

When you limit yourself to sedentary practice, you are instilling a belief that you must create ideal external circumstances to be whole, a belief that creates a struggle between daily life and awareness, because external circumstances will never match the mind's idea of a perfect meditation condition. With a simple change of attitude, backed by a flexible meditation approach, there is no need for such struggle.

You can be incredibly aware and whole while in active, daily life. In fact, don't be surprised if you find yourself experiencing some of the following phenomena associated with deeper brainwave patterns even while in motion:

- Moments of perfect blissful clarity
- Spontaneous insights and solutions to problems that had previously plagued you
- Relaxation as long-held, unresolved mental/emotional issues and traumas begin to melt away
- Incredible engagement with the present, such that time seems to speed up, making hours feel like minutes — yet, amazingly, time can also seem to slow down when you are in tricky life situations, giving you more time to navigate those difficult moments consciously
- Enhanced physical sensations such as feeling your pulse throughout your entire body, knowing when someone is staring at you from behind, or feeling at one with your environment
- Levels of intimacy and sexual pleasure beyond what you have ever experienced before
- Inexplicable experiences of synchronicity
- Profound visionary states
- Transcendent sense of oneness with the universe

Because TEM has no dogma or fixed form, and because it is based purely on awareness principles and the natural characteristics of the human body, it is highly flexible and applies well to any situation. In fact, many of my students are longtime practitioners and teachers of other forms of meditation. They report one of the greatest benefits of the TEM approach to be that it blends extremely well with whatever it is that they are currently practicing — and amplifies that thing.

With flexibility in mind, it is my hope that practitioners of other forms of meditation take what they find beneficial from the TEM approach and, if they like, use it to enhance what they are already doing. For people who are new to meditation, have no concern about difficulty, for you will quickly discover how easy the Warrior's Meditation is. Time and again, I have seen that even children can meditate easily with it. In fact, they have an easier time of it than adults, who tend to overthink the process.

Let's begin our exploration!

Part I

Principles of Meditation

What is meditation? Many people tend to equate meditation with a certain disciplined practice that entails sitting cross-legged in silence, with eyes closed. Readers might be surprised to find that there are many ways to tap into the vibrant awareness of meditation, and they are not all equally efficient.

Almost every meditation has a specific fixed form that defines it. The problem with form-based definitions of meditation is that they can cause us to value the steps and the traditions over the awareness that meditation was originally aimed to reveal.

To avoid the trap of form and tradition, I will define meditation not as a form but, instead, as a state of vibrant clarity that comes of deeply integrated present moment awareness. How we get to that vibrant present awareness, in my estimation, is less important than the direct experience of vibrant clarity.

To transcend form and tradition, we must first isolate the principles of awareness. Of course, to isolate principles of awareness, it is helpful to know a little about the state of the brain during meditation, as compared with the state of the brain when not meditated. The differences are reflected in measurable brainwaves.

In Part I, we explore the first brainwave associated with meditation and contrast it with the brainwave associated with thought and daily activity. We will use two key exercises, vagal breathing and fixed-point focus, to discover the difference between our regular, stress-inducing brainwave patterns, known as beta waves, and contrast them with alpha waves, the first brainwaves that show up when we are meditated.

Practicing the exercises in Part I will not only demonstrate to you, through your own experience, the differences between these two brainwave states, but it will also serve to isolate vital awareness principles that, once understood, will enhance your understanding of any form of meditation you practice. Once you have embodied the principles of awareness deeply enough through repeated experience, you will find that you are free of meditation forms and are naturally in a state of vibrant awareness throughout your day.

As I stated in the previous chapter, beta waves are expressed when the brain is focused and engaged in mental activities. For example, a normal conversation would stimulate the typical beta wave state in the average person. By comparison, arguments, speeches, and debates would stimulate a high beta wave state.

For most people, unless we are at rest, the brain is constantly generating measurable beta waves. When at rest, the brain is generally emitting alpha waves, which are slower and higher in amplitude. Alpha represents a nonaroused state, so a basic calming meditation would be reflective of alpha.

Once we have isolated, experienced, and established a basic understanding of the differences between beta wave and alpha wave and how those states relate to meditation, and we have established an understanding of the essential principles of meditation, we will begin our exploration of the basic TEM practice, the Warrior's Meditation.

I believe that with some experience you will appreciate the incredible ease and flexibility of the Warrior's Meditation. You can then use it as a standalone method, if you like, or as an adjunct to other methods that may suit you personally. Practicing the exercises found in Part 1 even a few times should be sufficient to ground your understanding of the essential principles that will free up your meditation practice.

Chapter 1

The Path of Concentration

Buddhists say that all forms of meditation derive from one of two approaches, Vipassana "insight" meditation or Samatha "purification" meditation. Of course, meditation stretches back far before the advent of Buddhism, but if we look at the underlying principles of Vipassana and Samatha, we can see that the main principles of those meditations are found in various forms of ancient as well as modern meditations.

Again, Vipassana translates into English as *insight*, whereas Samatha translates as *purification*. A good word to summarize the key principle of Vipassana is *awareness*, whereas with Samatha, a similar term might be *concentration*.

According to the Buddhist sutras, the Buddha taught both Vipassana and Samatha in tandem, not referring to them as meditation modalities, but instead stating that they were qualities that resulted from the practice of proper meditation, and that both qualities were necessary for liberation.

Unfortunately, though most schools of Buddhism claim that they teach the true meditation of Buddha, in actuality no one knows what the original method was, for no original writings exist. Nonetheless, many modern expressions of Buddhism have separated Vipassana and Samatha and codified them into specific meditation forms. Most schools practice one or the other method, with the vast majority using Samatha concentration-based meditations primarily, which fit easily into a religious culture, wherein the focal point could be a sutra, a prayer, or a religious image or name.

Vipassana could be considered a less intensely focused form of meditation than Samatha. By comparison, in Samatha you attempt to concentrate to the exclusion all but the focal point, whereas Vipassana is a little more fluid. For example, concentration schools might have you focus on a candle flame or a certain word (mantra) that you repeat in your mind or say aloud to exclusion of all other awareness, whereas mindfulness meditation might have you focus on the path of the breath and the comings and goings of thought while remaining detached from them.

Beyond Buddhism, we find that of all meditations known around the world, the vast majority of them falls into the concentration category, with distinctions largely found in their specific focal point, their tradition, and their culture.

As for the principle of Vipassana/awareness, we can look to mindfulness meditation, which is a secular derivative of Buddhist practices. The basic mindfulness meditation focuses awareness on the breath. Because breath travels through the body with its own natural ebb and flow, our awareness is a little more expansive than it would be if we focus on a mantra, for example.

From the TEM perspective, the basic Samatha/concentration and Vipassana/awareness meditations are not so different, in that both forms are exclusive in their attention. Samatha schools advise total exclusive attention or focus, whereas Vipassana schools are by comparison a little less exclusive. The similarity, from the TEM perspective, is that both approaches advise exclusive attention.

The reason these schools are exclusive in their meditative focus is that if you relax into focus on one thing long enough the mind will quiet and there will be a breakthrough into a deeper awareness.

When I first practiced meditation as a teen, just such a breakthrough happened to me. It took a lot of sustained attention for a long period of time, but it did happen. The only problem was that I was not able to get back to that place of vibrant awareness again using the concentration approach.

Of course, it is possible to have exactly the same type of enlightening breakthrough with any type of meditation, but truth be told, breakthrough experiences are rare even for dedicated meditators using the concentration approach. Some people can practice diligently for their entire lives and not have the breakthrough experience, whereas others will have a breakthrough the very first time and never again.

Once we have had such a breakthrough, we tend to hunger for it again, and if it doesn't come, we might be inclined to give up in frustration. Of course, a lot of us might not be interested in an enlightenment experience but are, instead, simply interested in improving the quality of our lives, reducing stress, improving our perspective, and so forth. Relaxed concentration is indeed a way to get there, but there is another path, one not about exclusive concentration — one that blends seamlessly with your active daily life.

Again, whether Samatha or Vipassana, traditional meditations are all exclusive in their awareness when compared to the TEM approach, which means they are concentration based. Understanding the principle of concentration through direct experience will give you a basis to understand the fundamental difference between the TEM approach and other approaches to meditation. To get you that foundational experience, we will design our own concentration-based meditation for you to practice now, based on the options that are traditionally available.

If we look at almost every type of meditation found around the world, we notice that they all have something in common, and that is concentration on something specific to the exclusion of all else. Zazen, seated meditation in Zen Buddhism, for example, focuses on maintaining proper physical structure of the body during meditation. Mindfulness meditation, meanwhile, focuses on maintaining awareness of the natural path of the breath during meditation. Mantra-based meditations —

17

Transcendental Meditation, commonly known as TM, and Christian meditation, for example — focus on repeating a spiritual word vocally or in the mind. Regardless of the country of origin, the religion, or the form of the meditation, all of them focus on something to the exclusion of all else.

Now, let's get some experience with concentration meditation. Select from the bullet list below the point of focus that you would like to meditate on (if you are already well versed in concentration-based meditation, feel free to skip to the heading on the next page, "Final Thoughts on Concentration Meditation"):

- An unwavering, upright seated posture
- Awareness of the breath
- A mind's eye–focus on a religious or sacred symbol
- The feeling between your closed eyes
- Mental repetition of a one-syllable word of your choosing, such as "peace," "love," "joy," et cetera
- Vocal repetition of a prayer of your choice

For our practice, we are going to follow the general guidelines that most meditation traditions advise.

Time

Set a timer for 15 minutes, so that you are less inclined to think about time during the meditation.

Place

Choose a warm, quiet, comfortable location where you will not be disturbed.

Positioning

Sit comfortably wherever you would like to practice, with your spine lightly erect but not overly stiff.

Eyes

Close the eyes or keep them just slightly open, but if they are open, do not allow them to focus on anything in the visual field.

Practice

The goal of your meditation practice here should be to maintain awareness upon your selected focal point, while being as relaxed as possible. When you notice that your mind wanders, and it is likely to from time to time, simply return your awareness to the focal point without any concern.

Do not be overly concerned with doing it right or wrong, for that concern will keep you from relaxing sufficiently to enter a meditative state. Simply keep to your chosen focal point and don't over think the process, something that adults are very prone to do.

Final Thoughts on Concentration Meditation

There is a reason that concentration meditation is found in almost every culture and spiritual practice around the world. In short, concentration meditation, if we are persistent, works.

Ideally, you enjoyed your first meditation. If you are like I was when I first started meditating, you might find that you want to meditate for more than fifteen minutes. If you have the time and you are enjoying concentration meditation, it is highly advised that you take all the time that you like to explore.

One of the challenges to concentration-based meditations is how easy it is to become bored or distracted as the brain tires from the effort required to concentrate. People who suffer from ADHD tend to find concentration meditations to be extremely difficult, as their attention jumps around almost constantly. The same difficulty is experienced by children, who quite understandably might begin to dislike meditation if they are forced to use a concentration-based method.

If you would like to explore concentration-based meditations in more depth, I have provided detailed instructions for how to perform seated Zen, mantra, and mindfulness meditations in the Ready Reference section. I recommend the exploration.

Chapter 2

Beyond Concentration

As we are not necessarily practicing meditation for religious purposes, there is no need to get caught up in the terminology, the religious aims, and the forms of traditional meditation. I referred to those things early to help the reader understand the origins of meditation and to see beyond the terminology, so that we can get to the liberating principles of meditation. That stated, to give these traditions their fair shake, I will explain just a bit more here before moving on to the principles that will free you of the forms.

Thanks to religious competitiveness and the tendency for human beings to cling to names and traditions, it can seem as if Samatha (concentration) and Vipassana (awareness) are totally separate practices, but there is a fair amount of overlap in the practice between these two principles, even though that overlap is rarely indicated by teachers.

It is wise to note that concentration and awareness are not totally separate things. For example, if you relax into concentration for a long enough period, a deep awareness can suddenly emerge. Relaxation, awareness, and insight can emerge through any meditative practice, but — and this is important — not all meditative practices are equally consistent in this regard.

Depending upon the individual and their life situation, some forms of meditation require a lot more effort to get the desired effect, and of course, all structured meditations have their limits, based upon the particular form. Such limitations include requirements for sitting, maintaining certain postures, hand gestures, tongue positions, closing the eyes, breathing in certain ways, chanting (vocally or nonvocally), et cetera.

It might be easy to understand why standing in the grocery line and chanting a mantra is ill-advised. Chanting in public is an antisocial activity, for it will cause other people to shy away from you, and rightly so. Anyone who is even slightly aware is, on some level, watching for danger, and if you can't even stand in a grocery line normally, that is a red flag to other people. If we are wise, we do not chant while in public. Thus, the belief that chanting is required to meditate limits us as to when we can apply the meditation.

Likewise, if we believe we have to sit down and close our eyes to find calm clarity, we are limited. For most people, though, there is no reason for such a limitation, other than the fact that we believe that meditation must be done in a certain way.

So long as we hold such beliefs, our development as individuals is greatly limited. To reach our potential as human beings, it is necessary to question beliefs, assumptions, teachers, and traditions. I am not suggesting that we should argue or be rude with our teachers, but it is wise to question and explore through our own experience to see what our current limitations are. Through questioning and exploring, little by little, we may find that former limitations begin to melt away.

Why do we believe that we can't be calm and clear while walking, while talking, while working? Maybe those circumstances are not actual limiting factors, as we have believed them to be. There is only one way to find out — challenge those assumptions over and over again. With continued exploration and practice, you will surely find you can do all of those things from a place of awareness.

The amazing thing about meditation is that, even with all the limits we have placed on the practice, people still gain tremendous benefit from it. Imagine how much more powerful meditation could be if we release ourselves from the strictures of concentration and form and, instead, embrace the liberating principles.

I am not knocking tradition here, for I have spent a great deal of my life training in the traditional martial and healing arts, where, just like in traditional meditation training, disciples are expected to discover the true process for themselves. Basically, I agree with the self-discovery approach, but I also feel that instructors should inform their students that they are responsible for exploring and refining their understanding of the path on their own. Although my teacher made a point to clearly state the requirements of personal exploration to each student, many teachers do not tell their students what is expected of them.

In the days of the Samurai, it was generally understood that disciples had to find their way through the curriculum without relying on the teacher to tell them things. In those days, the path to mastery was described as Shuhari. The word *Shuhari* consists of three distinct Chinese characters, 守破離, which describe the order that the path to mastery should take.

Shu (守) translates into English as "protect" or "obey." At the Shu stage, disciples are to obey and follow the guidelines and techniques of the curriculum to gain a basic experiential understanding. We could think of Shu as the training-wheel stage.

Ha (破) translates into English as "detach" or "digress." The Ha stage of learning requires questioning the curriculum by exploring beyond the established techniques. In the Ha stage, the training wheels are removed.

Ri (離), which translates into English as "leave" or "separate," means to surrender to a totally aware yet natural way of being, free from techniques. Very, very few individuals ever make it to the Ri stage of any practice. We could refer to Ri as mastery.

Ri is a stage that cannot be realized by beginners, for when beginners surrender to a natural way of being, what emerges is not awareness but habit, which is the accumulation of unconscious, less-functional patterns over a lifetime. For proper Ri to emerge, a profound awareness must be sustained such that dysfunctional, unconscious patterns become conscious, and are transformed through the Ha stage, so that the individual then becomes unconsciously functional — Ri. What emerges at the Ri stage is no longer just regurgitation of habits and techniques, but is instead something new and inspired — complete.

Many, if not most, modern day meditation teachers are actually still at some level of the Shu stage, and because they are still bound by form, they do not see the vista that lies beyond the curriculum. They do not see that they are actually imprisoned by the techniques and the teaching, which initially helped them but now are weighing them down.

This critique is aimed not just at ancient traditions — for humans, regardless of era, can become comfortable with forms and theories, and addicted to them. In scientific and academic worlds, it is not unusual to ostracize an outsider who challenges a well-established theory. Ludwig Boltzmann, for example, developed formulae that explained the properties of atoms as the basis of the physical nature of matter. His theory also disproved the accepted theories of the time. Boltzmann was dismissed by authorities in his field, and ultimately he committed suicide after years of fighting to gain traction for his theory. Three years after Boltzmann committed suicide, Ernest Rutherford proved him right by discovering the nucleus of an atom.

Some degree of skepticism is important, but so is exploration. To dismiss and discourage exploration is unwise, but it is part of human nature to do so, and intelligence has never been a reliable failsafe against the lure of previously accepted knowledge, as some of the most rational individuals on the planet — scientists — have shown time and again.

Free yourself of biases by being curious, by exploring. You'll discover that it is quite empowering and fun to meditate as an exploration, not just as a discipline. In fact, I would suggest that any meditation wherein you are not exploring is not actual meditation at all, because you are not fully engaged, not fully paying attention, not coming at each moment afresh — which means you are in a beta wave state.

24

To encourage exploration, once you get the hang of the basics of TEM, I suggest exploring and testing, again and again, to see how you might stretch your limits. If you already have an established meditation practice, I recommend that you explore that practice again, as if for the very first time.

Many teachers reject breaking with tradition to explore. Do not be concerned, for there is no need to argue with your teacher or fight against a tradition. Just explore on your own and move forward in a life-enriching way, for that is the best way to make a positive change in your life and in the world. Have fun with meditation.

Regarding Shuhari, I suspect most traditions actually teach the concept, possibly using other terminology. The problem is that so few practitioners go through all these phases, thanks to the pace of the modern world and the failure of traditions to adapt their teaching modality. We just don't have the time anymore, so the path of Shuhari, even if instructed as a concept, is generally not lived.

When the main job of the Samurai was to train themselves, they had almost all day, every day, to explore and discover. The same could be said of monks. Under those ideal circumstances, it might not be necessary to point out principles to disciples. But in modern life, people don't have as much time to dedicate to training, exploring, and discovering, and as a result, the principles have largely been overlooked and forgotten, leaving us stuck to form and tradition.

Regardless of the teaching, however, we must all begin our practice with form, and that is true of TEM, as well. The difference is that with TEM, you learn the principles at the beginner's stage, so that the form becomes extremely flexible for you in practice, which rapidly takes you to the Ha stage of exploration that can, in turn, rapidly take you to the stage of inspired freedom, Ri.

Chapter 3

Shifting to Alpha

The first scientifically measurable shift that takes place when we enter into meditation is in brainwaves. They go from a goal-oriented, aroused state, which coincides with beta wave, to alpha, which indicates a resting, relaxed state. In general, it takes less than a minute for the brain to shift from beta wave to alpha wave during meditation.

The longer we spend in engaged meditation, the deeper is the alpha wave, which can then shift into theta, delta, and possibly even gamma wave, which represent still deeper awareness possibilities and health benefits.

As it turns out, any form of meditation can shift your brainwave to alpha. In fact, if you just sit observing your breath for one minute, you will probably enter alpha wave. The same shift is also likely to occur if you pray or chant for one minute. Armed with the knowledge that any meditation can take us into alpha, we can combine that understanding to come up with a simple method to efficiently shift our brains to alpha wave even during daily activity.

One such method is vagal breathing. Vagal breathing is a very easy process, which for most people will require no more than two breaths to make the shift into alpha wave if done properly. Considering that some readers may carry more anxiety and stress than others, and that a few attempts will be required just to familiarize yourself with the process, we should be sure to do at least six vagal breaths, so that everyone makes the shift to alpha.

Although we will not be relying on breath methods once we are familiar with the Warrior's Meditation, vagal breathing will give you an idea of how easy it is to shift from beta wave to alpha. Once you can recognize when the shift occurs, we can explore more applicable approaches that can blend seamlessly with your daily life.

Before we get to vagal breathing, here's what you need to know about the vagus nerve: the name of the vagus nerve was inspired by the term *vagabond*, which means "wanderer," because the vagus nerve, which is the longest of the cranial nerves, has sensory fibers that connect your brainstem to your visceral organs. The vagus nerve controls the parasympathetic nervous system, counteracts the symptoms of an overactive sympathetic nervous system, namely stress, anxiety, and other fight-flight-freeze adrenal responses, including some forms of depression.

The vagus nerve manages a vast array of vital functions by conveying motor and sensory impulses to the organs. Until quite recently, medical science perceived no connection between the immune-system and the nervous system, because immune cells float freely in the body, whereas nerve cells are fixed in location. Because of this seeming disconnect between the nervous system and immune function, the scientific and medical community assumed that the nervous system could play no role in immune function. However, a growing body of research by Kevin Tracey — neurosurgeon and president of the Feinstein Institute for Medical Research in Manhasset, N.Y. — is indicating that stimulation of the vagus nerve may be a powerful means of treating chronic inflammation and so-called incurable diseases (Pavlov and Tracey).

Tracey experimented with rats to determine whether electrical stimulation of the vagus nerve would alleviate inflammation. He anesthetized a rat, cut an incision in its neck, and delivered several one-second electrical pulses to the rat's exposed vagus nerve. After he stitched the cut, he administered a bacterial protein that triggers inflammation in mammals.

After an hour, there should have been rampant inflammation, but instead, inflammation was blocked by 75 percent. Tracey discovered that all information signals between the brain and the rest of the body, including inflammation, come and go as electrical signals.

So how does this vagus nerve discovery relate to the breath? Tracey used electricity to stimulate the vagus nerve, but we can use the breath to do so. Wim Hof has shown that practitioners of his breathing method are immune to toxic proteins administered into their blood (Kox et al.).

Preliminary studies of Hof's method at the Radboud University Medical Center in the Netherlands indicate that these techniques can temporarily suppress an inappropriate immune response. The same effects have been found in other, similar breathing methods.

Peter Pikkers and his PhD student, Matthis Kox, tested blood samples from Hof and students trained in the method for indicators of inflammation before their breathing exercises and meditations and after an 80-minute full-body ice bath. The results showed greatly reduced levels of proteins associated with the immune response.

Pikkers and Kox used another experiment to test Hof's innate immune system response. The innate immune system distinguishes the body's own cells from invading cells and eliminates the intruders.

They injected an endotoxin meant to stimulate immune response. Most subjects experience fever, headaches, and shivering after exposure to the injected poison, as well as elevated levels of signaling proteins called cytokines. Hof did not suffer any of the negative symptoms and had half as many cytokines as control subjects. His students who later took the same test had a response similar to Hof's.

I believe the link to be the vagus nerve, which is being stimulated by certain types of breathing. Although much more research remains necessary to confirm why these breathing methods create the incredibly beneficial immune responses that they do, the body of research on the vagus nerve and how it affects health is growing.

As Kevin Tracey showed, the vagus nerve, which connects to every organ except adrenal glands, can prevent inflammation. When the vagus nerve gets an inflammation signal, it notifies the brain. The result is the release of anti-inflammatory neurotransmitters that regulate immune response. Vagal breathing and similar methods help the immune system have an appropriate response to pathogens.

The vagus nerve also communicates between your gut and your brain through electrical impulses to clarify your "gut feeling" or intuition. If the communication is clear, our gut feeling will be much more accurate than it would be if our nervous system is over-reactive or under-reactive.

A study conducted at the University of Virginia has shown that stimulation of the vagus nerve strengthens memory (Hassert et al.). The stimulation triggered norepinephrine to be released into the amygdala, which consolidates memories. The effect works in both rats and humans and suggests that avenues through the vagus nerve may offer new treatment of conditions like Alzheimer's disease.

Just as the vagus nerve is intimately connected with all the organs and regulates their function, it also regulates the heart-rate through electrical impulses to muscle tissue in the right atrium. The result is a release of acetylcholine, which slows the pulse. As Tibetan monks have repeatedly shown, they can slow the heartbeat through their breathing — and so can you.

The vagus nerve initiates the body's relaxation response. Most of us have an overstimulated sympathetic nervous system, which results in near-constant release of the stress hormones cortisol and adrenaline into the bloodstream. Proper breathing can stimulate the vagus nerve to tell your body to relax through the release of acetylcholine, prolactin, vasopressin, and oxytocin.

Regular stimulation of the vagus nerve has been shown to drastically reduce and/or stop symptoms of rheumatoid arthritis, hemorrhagic shock, and other serious inflammatory diseases that were previously thought to be incurable.

We are on the cusp of new treatments using the qualities of the vagus nerve. But to Tibetan monks, there is probably nothing surprising in these new findings, for they have been using the breath to stimulate the vagus nerve as a means of treating inflammation for, perhaps, thousands of years.

Here's how to perform vagal breathing:

Aim

The aim of this exercise is to not only make the shift from beta wave to alpha but also to notice when that shift occurs.

Preliminaries

Before we begin the vagal breathing exercise, take note of the state of your mind and the feeling of your body. There is no need to try to change the feeling in the body before doing the exercise, for the entire point of the exercise is to notice a change during the exercise.

Here are some questions to ask yourself (it might be helpful to measure on a scale from 1 to 10, with 10 being the highest):
- What are your tension levels?
- How much anxiety do you feel?
- How heavy do you feel?
- How calm do you feel?

Time

Set your timer for fifteen minutes to get a good experiential understanding of vagal breathing.

Position

Intense vagal stimulation can cause a rapid blood-pressure drop resulting in a potential fainting spell. Apart from the danger of falling down, no other negative side effects stem from vagal stimulation. Therefore, for this exercise, I recommend that you sit down, without using a backrest.

Eyes

Eyes closed initially until you gain a good sense of the process, then open if you like.

Breathing Method

Take in a completely full breath and hold it, while using the breath to stretch the lungs in a way that feels really good. By repositioning your abdomen, spine, shoulders, and neck, you will find that you can move pressure of the air around in the lungs.

Play with the pressure in the lungs by stretching the lungs to find which directional pressure feels best for you in the moment. If it feels good to stretch in this way for a few seconds and then shift to another direction, and then another, that is fine.

Don't think too much about this process, for with any meditation feeling is the key to a powerful experience. Here is a link to video I made that demonstrates vagal breathing:
https://richardlhaight.com/vagal

Stretch the lungs with the pressure of your breaths for as long as it feels good, then exhale in a way that also feels deeply satisfying. Exhale, pause, and relax for as long as feels good before taking several relaxed recovery breaths as you like. Take another stretching breath as soon as you feel ready to do so. Repeat this breathing process for five minutes.

The key with vagal breathing is not being super willful, but instead paying attentive to what feels good at each stage of the process. If vagal breathing is done properly, which means paying attention to what feels really good, the brain will shift from beta to alpha wave during the first breath. With fifteen minutes of practice, vagal breathing should noticeably drain tension from your body and create a warm, clear, calm feeling.

Dealing with Distraction

If the mind wanders, which is highly unlikely if you are enjoying the process, just bring awareness back to breathing without any concern.

Assessment

With vagal breathing, making the shift from beta to alpha is very easy for most people. Although an easy method, vagal breathing is a powerful first step in the meditative process.

Did you notice when the shift from beta to alpha occurred? If not, get back into beta wave, so that you can re-experience vagal breathing to note when the shift occurs. There are several easy ways to get back into beta. Hyper-focusing the mind to solve a problem, negative thinking, and lying are sure ways to stimulate a high beta wave. Another easy way to get back into beta for beginners is to move the body vigorously — for example, stomping your feet and flailing your arms.

Once back in beta, do the vagal breathing exercise again to notice the shift to alpha. For most people, the shift to alpha will occur within the first fulfilling breath.

Once you are in alpha wave take the assessment again, scaling each question from 1 to 10.

- What are your tension levels?

- How much anxiety do you feel?
- How heavy do you feel?
- How calm do you feel?

If, after taking six vagal breaths, you have not noticed any clear change in feeling, then that means you are being blocked by something probably related to your life pattern. Whatever the issue is, it is surely negatively affecting your health in profound ways. In all likelihood, your body is not recovering efficiently when you are at rest or while sleeping. In that case, you may be stuck in beta even during times of inactivity, which can have tremendous short-term and long-term negative effects on your physical, mental, and emotional well-being.

Correcting the blockage is of utmost importance, for everything in your life will probably improve through the correction. If you are one of the rare individuals who could not make the shift to alpha through vagal breathing, please do not worry, for we will discuss potential blocking issues later in the book to help you find a powerful, holistic solution.

Final Notes on Shifting to Alpha

Vagal breathing is a quick, almost sure-fire way to shift from beta to alpha wave. That said, from the TEM perspective, this breath method — or any breath method — can keep us from some degree of full engagement in active daily life because it is hard to talk to someone, for example, while vagal breathing, so we will make only selective use of this technique. For example, vagal breathing can be a great exercise when you first get out of bed, when on the toilet, or during any other moment where you are inactive, physically or mentally. Vagal breathing is also a great exercise to do if you find yourself getting nervous or upset about something, for it is likely to calm your nervous system, and therefore your mind, considerably within just a few breaths.

Note: I do not recommend doing vagal breathing while standing passively or operating a motor-vehicle because you can faint when the blood-pressure drops on the exhale. Aside from the potential injury from a fall, there are no known negative health effects of vagal breathing. On the contrary, all evidence to date suggests that vagal breathing is incredibly beneficial.

Chapter 4

Differentiating Alpha States

From our explorations in the previous chapter, we know that we can consciously make the shift from the stressful beta wave state to alpha. With our newfound ability, we can refine the process by getting a better sense of what is happening in the brain, when the shift from beta to alpha occurs, and what stimulates that shift. That awareness will provide us with more flexibility in our meditations.

In 1969 Herbert Krugman monitored the brainwaves of people while watching TV and found that it took less than one minute of television viewing for a person's brainwaves to switch from beta to mainly alpha. When individuals stopped watching TV and read instead, their brainwaves switched back primarily to beta waves. Krugman was interested in researching the brain to maximize the impact of advertising. Krugman's research is still largely used to inform the advertising industry (Krugman and Hartley).

The thing to know about alpha is that it does not always indicate awareness. Yes, alpha is generally the brainwave associated with meditation, but it is also the brainwave associated with daydreaming or watching TV. Hopefully, we understand that our TV watching time is not the transformative equal to time spent in meditation.

Now that we know meditation and TV watching stimulate similar brainwave patterns, it is vital that we explore the difference between the experience of meditation and that of watching TV to understand how meditation affects us differently from watching TV.

As Krugman's experiment demonstrated, it takes less than a minute for a person's brainwaves to shift from beta to alpha when they sit down to watch TV, so we will be mindful of that fact and conduct our experiment for five minutes to increase the chances that you will successfully make the shift from beta to alpha and back again during the exercise.

The purpose of the experiment will be to distinguish a conscious, meditative alpha state from an unconscious, TV-watching alpha state, for they are experientially quite different.

Unconscious Alpha Experiment

For this experiment, I use the terms *conscious* and *unconscious* to differentiate two distinct states of alpha. By conscious I do not mean just your daily wakeful mind, and by unconscious I do not mean sleeping or coma-like states. Instead, I use the term *conscious* to indicate a highly aware perception and *unconscious* to indicate an awake, yet inattentive, dull, habitual state of mind.

This experiment will focus on noticing the difference between alpha wave states of TV watching and the alpha wave state achieved through meditation. The conscious alpha of meditation is compatible with what is achieved through vagal breathing, so since we have already learned vagal breathing we will use it as our means of shifting to conscious alpha during this exercise.

To have a successful experiment, we must first be sure that we begin in a beta wave state. To get into a beta wave state, we can do some mental calculations, which almost guarantee that the brain is emitting a strong beta wave. Once we are clearly in beta, we will watch TV to shift the brain into alpha wave.

We will be using a timer set to five minutes for TV watching. Be sure to prepare the video that you intend to watch before conducting the experiment, so that all you will need to do is press the play button for it to initiate. I recommend watching a video that you enjoy, but not an action, suspense, or horror genre, as those are likely to trigger stress and keep you in beta wave. Of course, we do not want to enter a conscious alpha state, so it is wise to avoid watching a meditation-related video.

Here are the steps to the experiment:

1. Set a timer for five minutes.
2. Stomp your feet, flail your arms, and do some mental calculations to be sure your brain is emitting beta waves. Mentally do these calculations to be sure your brain is emitting beta waves. It doesn't actually matter if you get the correct answer or not, but it does matter that you do the mental work to derive whatever answer you come up with, for the effort will put you into beta wave.
   - $11 \times 9 =$
   - $72 - 23 =$
   - $7 + 15 - 3 =$
3. Once the calculations are complete, take note of how you feel.
4. Start your timer and begin watching your video.
5. When the timer sounds, take note of the difference between how your body feels after watching video for five minutes as compared to how you felt after doing the mental calculations.
6. If you are unsure of the change in feeling, redo the experiment until you can notice the difference.

Generally speaking, you will note that when the brain is emitting alpha wave, the body is more relaxed than when in beta, which is a somewhat tense, goal-oriented state.

As I stated earlier, even though watching video puts us into alpha wave, that state of induced relaxation is not the same as that of meditation, for when watching video we are not consciously aware. Instead, we are in an absorbed, dreamlike state, which we will explore more in the next chapter.

Now let's try the next experiment, which is meant to give us a baseline of experience with conscious alpha.

Conscious Alpha Experiment

As we discussed earlier, shifting to alpha from beta generally takes less than a minute for the average person when watching TV or when meditating.

We are going to run the same experiment again to contrast the feeling of beta with the feeling of alpha, but this time, instead of watching TV, we will practice vagal breathing as we did in the previous chapter.

Here are the steps to the experiment:

1. Set a timer for five minutes.
2. Vigorously move your body and mentally do these calculations to put your brain into beta wave state.
   - $12 \times 8 =$
   - $71 - 21 =$
   - $3 + 5 - 7 =$
3. Take note of how you feel immediately after calculating.
4. Start your timer and begin vagal breathing.
5. When the timer sounds, take note of the difference between your bodily feeling after vagal breathing for five minutes as compared to how you felt after doing the vigorous movements and mental calculations.
6. If you are unsure of the change in feeling, redo the experiment until you can notice the difference.

During both the unconscious (video-watching) and conscious (vagal-breathing) shift to alpha wave, a change in feeling certainly occurred. The key is to be aware of the difference between conscious and unconscious alpha feeling. Generally speaking, a conscious alpha state will feel relaxed, open, and aware.

If you didn't notice the difference between video watching and vagal stimulation, do the experiments again a few times until you isolate the difference. It may take a few attempts before you notice — just keep at it.

When you notice the difference between conscious and unconscious alpha, then you have gotten your first glimpse into what meditation is. The key to meditation is conscious feeling, which is awareness, and once you know that, you are no longer limited to a set meditation form.

Final Thoughts on Alpha versus Beta Wave States

For modern people in developed nations, 90-plus percent of our waking time is spent in beta wave state, because we are thinking and focusing so much. Beta wave is a stress-generating brainwave to which we have been habituated by our safe, goal-oriented modern world of squares, angles, and edges. In our world, exclusive attention is encouraged through reading and constant thinking. Because there are no tigers around that might eat us, awareness is not required. The result is that, although we lead safer lives than do hunter-gatherers, we are highly anxious by comparison.

Hunter-gatherers spend most of their time in alpha wave because awareness is vital to their survival. They understand that the focused mind is very poor at detecting subtlety and movement in the environment. They know that awareness of subtle change and movement are the means by which one has the highest chance of success when you have to hunt for food and not get lost, bitten by a snake, eaten by a predator, or fall off a cliff. That subtle awareness is rooted in a sustained conscious alpha state.

A large part of why we, in the modern world, are so prone to stress, frustration, anxiety, depression, self-absorption, and feelings of loneliness is that our lifestyles tend to be disconnected from the rhythms and requirements of nature, and that out-of-sync lifestyle has engrained a profoundly unhealthy neural pattern.

Now that we know of our deficit, we can begin to make the necessary correction in our lives, by intending each day to be in conscious alpha states, even if only for short durations.

Chapter 5

The Awareness Paradox

Now that we are aware of the difference between conscious alpha and unconscious alpha, the next step is to isolate vital principles of meditation, so that we may free ourselves from the limitations of concentration-based meditations.

In this chapter, we are going to conduct some experiments on ourselves that will reveal the awareness paradox, which is a principle that frees up our practice, allowing us to meditate with eyes open and, with some practice, while on the move.

All concentration meditations aim to focus on one point to the exclusion of all other awareness. The point of focus could be most anything, but for our focal point, we will use either a candle flame or a fixed point on the wall.

Fixed-Point Focus Experiment

The intention in this experiment is to focus our vision completely on a candle flame, a single point on the wall, or other fixed point of your choosing, to exclusion for an extended period.

We're going to conduct this experiment at least twice. The first time that you do the fixed-point focus exercise, set your timer for five minutes.

While seated comfortably and facing a wall, or at a table for the candle method, select a fixed point on the wall several feet in front of you, or light a candle and place it on the table a few feet in front of you. Start your timer and begin staring at the candle or the fixed point on the wall.

The goal is to try your best to see only the fixed point or candle flame and nothing else, while being careful not to squint in the attempt to avoid seeing the larger picture. Before reading on, please do the experiment.

So, what did you notice?

Most people, when I ask this question, say that they became calmer during this experiment. Don't worry in the least if you became anxious or did not experience calm during the experiment, for that is not its primary purpose.

What this exercise really demonstrates is that you can't help but see the entire peripheral field of vision when you are consciously aware and your eyes are open. The paradox is that the very attempt to exclude sensory awareness means that you are consciously aware, and a conscious individual cannot help but be aware of the entire visual field.

During your first attempt, you may not have realized that you were actually seeing the entire visual field while trying not to see it. Don't have the least concern if you didn't notice the paradox during the first experiment. To clear up the matter, we're going to run this same experiment again, but this time using a stopwatch rather than a timer.

Start your stopwatch and begin staring to exclusion, and observe how long it takes before you notice that you cannot exclude the total visual field.

Ideally, you noticed right away that you can't fail to see the entire visual field. Similar to when someone tells you not to think of purple monkeys, you are almost certain to think of them, you cannot help but see the entire visual field while trying not to see the entire field. This point may, at first glance, seem trivial, but soon you will realize that it is the untold secret to powerful, flexible, free meditation.

How does the principle work?

Think of all the times that you've read a book but thought you saw nothing beyond the edges of the book or the specific sentence you were reading. Or, if you are not a reader, think about all the times that you watched a movie and failed to notice anything beyond the screen. The truth is you did see, but you don't remember. Allow me to explain.

Your eyes see everything within the visible light spectrum that comes into your visual field — which includes the entire movie screen or book, plus and everything that is outside the edges of those mediums but within the capacity for your eyes to potentially see. You simply don't remember what your eyes saw.

You can verify what I am saying by using this book. While reading this sentence, simply choose not to see anything beyond the edges of the book. Be sure not to cheat by moving your face so close to the book's text that you physically can't see beyond the edges even with your peripheral vision. As you read, you will notice that you can't help but to see beyond the book.

Could you understand the text you were reading? Some of you may be surprised to find that you cannot understand the text when you are aware of what is happening in the room beyond the text. After practicing the Warrior's Meditation for a sufficient time, you may discover that, with a little practice, reading while being spatially aware isn't so difficult.

How does this experiment relate to meditation?

The experiment demonstrates the difference between when we are consciously aware and when we are not. When we are consciously aware, we can't help but perceive what comes into us through our senses. Only when we are in a semi-unconscious, dreamlike state — which can include watching movies, reading books, being absorbed in our inner narratives, mental projections of the future or the past, or any other means of distraction from present awareness — are we unable to recall or make use of the information outside the target of our focus, even though our senses are taking in that extra information.

We can begin to untangle the mystery of perception by observing the two hemispheres of the brain and how they function to provide two equal, yet distinct, perceptions of reality. Ninety percent of the population is right-handed, and for those individuals the left hemisphere is a serial processing brain, while the right hemisphere is a parallel processing brain. For my explanation of the hemispheres, I will use the average person as our example, being mindful that for some individuals the hemispheres are actually reversed (left-handed individuals are good examples of how the functions of the hemispheres may be reversed).

For the ninety percent of the population who are right handed, the sense of self, time, the logical mind, language abilities, and their access to specific knowledge is primarily located in the left hemisphere, which is the serial processing brain, whereas their spatial awareness, creativity, bodily awareness, et cetera are primarily located in the right hemisphere, the parallel processing brain.

The serial processor (left hemisphere) can process only one conscious action at a time, which is a great limitation. The strength of the serial processor is that it is good at focusing to get a highly detailed perception of its chosen object. Concentration, a primary talent of the serial processor, is necessary for human survival, but it drains energy and creates stress to the body. What the serial processing hemisphere lacks is contextual awareness of anything outside the point of focus.

The Samurai understood that focus and thinking are energy-intensive processes which cause slower combat response times. The Samurai considered thinking to be a function of "mind." Through training aimed at ever more efficiency, the Samurai found that they could access a state of "no mind," which was much more efficient on the battlefield, so they put special effort into gaining more conscious access to "no mind," with the aim of eventually being able to access the strengths of "no mind" unconsciously.

As it turns out, they were training themselves to strategically access the powers of parallel processing (right hemisphere). The parallel processor can process multiple pieces of information at once at speeds much higher than the serial processor, but at lower definition.

Although Samurai knew how to consciously access the parallel processor through meditation, it is unlikely that they knew which part of the brain was actually doing the work, something we now know. Of course, to gain the functionality that the Samurai valued, knowing which part of the brain was doing the work was not required.

Left-handed people may be tempted to think that they are accessing the parallel processing hemisphere more than right handed people, but as I stated, the hemispheres can be reversed, so a left-handed person is usually accessing the serial processing, thinking mind and sense of self just as right-handed people do.

This structuring means that, if we are untrained, regardless of whether we are left-handed or right-handed, our daily experience is dominated by the thinking, sense-of-self-generating hemisphere, regardless of its location in our skulls. We know this is true because left-handedness does not relieve individuals of the sense of self or give them any leg up regarding movement or meditation.

Now that we've become familiar with the serial processing hemisphere, let's explore the parallel processing hemisphere in more depth. As I stated, the parallel processor, unlike the serial processor, processes more than one thing at a time, yet at much greater speeds and lower resolution than the serial processor does.

Generally speaking, the parallel processor functions as the sensory warning system, for it constantly monitors the information coming through the senses, even if our daily waking window of perception is not always aware of all that information.

The parallel processor does not perceive linearly, as the serial processor does. Instead it decodes information much more rapidly but in abstract ways that are rich with meaning. The perceptions of the parallel processing brain are very difficult for the serial processor brain to understand.

The parallel processor, among other things, governs awareness of the body as well as bodily movement. Dream and sleep states are examples of some of the meandering, self-distorted, nonlinear perceptions of the parallel processing hemisphere.

What the elite Samurai discovered was that they could, through conscious awareness training, become more in tune with the parallel processor, so that they could make use of its information at speeds well beyond that of the thinking mind, improving awareness, movement quality, and efficiency.

Although the elite Samurai were probably motivated by the need for heightened efficiency on the battlefield, their training opened up an avenue of communication between the conscious and subconscious mind, and in so doing, not only did their awareness and martial skills increase, so too did the quality of their lives improve. Many such Samurai became known as "sword saints," for their vastly superior abilities over the average Samurai of ancient Japan. Kamiizumi Ise no Kami, the founder of Shinkage-ryu, was widely considered to be a sword saint.

In a way, the fixed-point focus experiment shows that, in fact, awareness can't help but be aware, for it has no capacity to exclude information. When we focus our minds while intentionally trying to exclude information, our very intention enables both hemispheres to coordinate and share information with our window of perception. How much informational recall we have depends largely upon practice.

One major problem comes with this focusing method. You will discover that such intense focus rapidly tires the brain. For a warrior, energy efficiency is of vital importance, so in TEM we take another route, which we will explore in chapters to come.

Part II

Natural Meditation Portals

As we experienced with the awareness paradox, concentration offers a means by which we may become aware of something more, if we wake up to that fact. Once we are thus aware, exclusive concentration is no longer required. Simply knowing about the paradox is freeing, for we no longer need to focus on the breath, a certain point in the body, a mantra, a single word, or anything in particular.

Simply realizing that we can't consciously exclude information from the senses opens up new, more flexible options with our meditations, allowing us to make use of our senses as a means of inner transformation and improved physical, mental, and emotional vitality.

Equipped with knowledge of the awareness paradox, we can begin exploring what the senses have to offer. What if there were a way to use the senses that brought about a tremendous state of meditative clarity? A path of meditation through the senses would liberate us from the need to focus, the need to sit, and the need to retreat from the world. No longer would we need to create an ideal external situation free of distractions in order to meditate.

The secret, I found, is to change the way we use our senses. With TEM, as a general rule of thumb, we do not focus our attention to exclusion but instead open awareness in all directions through all senses.

Counterintuitively, opening up all the senses without bias allows tremendous awareness of the internal as well as the external, which brings about a sense of connection to all of life, for our sense of proprioception (the sense of where our bodies begin and end in space) no longer feels hard and fast. Instead, it somehow feels permeable. This open feeling results in greater calm and clarity. Opening up the senses to a broader awareness changes the brain, creating more perceptual flexibility, greater insight, and better health than we would otherwise have. Counterintuitively, when the sense of proprioception becomes transparent, our movement quality increases.

In Part II, we explore each sense individually to gain greater awareness of how each sense can be used as a meditative portal.

Chapter 6

Conscious Sight

It may come as a surprise that science still does not have an agreed upon theory as to how sight works. Although we know much about how vision works, some aspects of visual perception remain mysterious.

The mystery of vision is that the eye is not capable of actually producing sufficiently high-quality images that could allow a human being to function in the world based upon the information that the eye provides. The most accepted conclusion is that the brain makes up for the lack of information by filling in the informational gaps with associated memory content.

According to this theory, much of what we think of as vision is actually biological assumption. If the theory is correct, it explains the many visual illusions that we humans are prone to experience.

If you're unfamiliar with visual illusions, run a quick internet search for the term "Optical Illusion" to get a sense of what I mean by the term.

What we know so far is that visual perception is the result of the eye receiving light from the visible spectrum, which reflects off objects. The eye sends electrical signals to the brain, which interprets the signals to create the images of the environment that we see in our minds.

In the human eye, light enters through the cornea and is then focused by the lens onto a light-sensitive membrane, called the retina, at the back of the eye. The retina contains photoreceptive cells called rods, which detect shades, and cones, which detect color. Rods and cones convert photons (light particles) into electrical signals. The electrical signals are transmitted by the optic nerve to various places in the brain, such as the central ganglia, the visual cortex, and the superior colliculus, where they are then interpreted and filled out with experiential association — memory.

For our meditation purposes, what we need to know about vision is that it can be divided into two types, foveal vision and peripheral vision.

Foveal vision is the high-definition, color-rich perception that comes directly down the focused line of sight. Foveal vision is the type of vision that modern humans are using almost to exclusion. When you read, you rely on foveal vision.

Peripheral vision is the field of visual perception that lies just outside the line of sight. You will notice that peripheral vision is low-definition, color-insensitive vision. The advantage of peripheral vision is that it is highly sensitive to shades and movement, which makes it useful as an awareness tool. Hunter-gatherers spend most of their active daily life paying attention to peripheral vision.

Peripheral Viewing Exercise

As we know from the awareness paradox, when we try to exclude information from our visual awareness, the very attempt ensures that we cannot exclude that information. Of course, focusing with the attempt to exclude information is taxing in terms of energy, so we are wise to find a more efficient way. The solution is to simply pay attention to the entire visual field from the outset. So, for our meditation purposes in this chapter, we will consciously direct attention to the entire visual field without any attempt to focus or exclude information.

Time

Set your timer for 15 minutes. Although the typical person's brain will shift to alpha after just one minute of peripheral viewing, practicing for 15 minutes will allow you to gain a much greater experiential understanding of the progressive changes that occur within you as a result of peripheral viewing.

Position

Just sit comfortably in a quiet location, where you will not be disturbed. This exercise can easily be practiced indoors or outdoors.

Aim

Our goal with this exercise is to make use of the peripheral field of vision to consciously access the parallel processor through an alpha brain wave. Doing so will not only make us more aware, it will also relieve stress and bring about a calm serenity. It will be helpful for you to note how you feel before doing this exercise. Also be sure to note when the shift to alpha occurs during the exercise, as well as how you feel once the exercise is complete.

Eyes

Gaze straight ahead and notice the entire visual field. The average person can see almost 200 degrees horizontally and about 100 degrees vertically, creating a "binocular"-shaped visual field. As stated earlier, the highest visual resolution will be at the center of the visual field, where there is full color and detail. If we focus our attention on the center of the visual field, that is called foveal vision.

Although we know from the awareness paradox that focusing on foveal vision with the intention to exclude information can take us into a state of conscious awareness, to conserve energy we must use a different method with our eyes.

What we want to do is keep our attention on the outer edges of our visual field, which is called peripheral vision. Peripheral vision is low resolution and low color, but is more sensitive to shades and motion. Paying attention to peripheral vision will give you more conscious access to the parallel processing brain, a trick that the Samurai discovered.

Stargazing provides a good example of the strength of peripheral vision. The enhanced motion sensitivity of peripheral vision helps us to detect the faint twinkling of the stars out of the corners of our eyes. When we try to focus on a dim star, counterintuitively, we find it harder to see.

Although most of us are unaware of it, information from the peripheral field of vision is constantly being fed to the brain. Because we are so focused on foveal vision, trying to gain specific information, we aren't typically aware of this entire field. Selective attention effectively blocks accessible memory of peripheral visual information that does not apply to our current activity. For example, when watching a movie at a theater, you are probably aware of the content on the movie screen only, without noticing what else is happening in the room before the screen.

I refer to movie watching as an unconscious activity because we tend to lack an awareness of our own presence while watching a movie. TEM aims for spatial and present-moment awareness. Of course, we may enjoy getting absorbed into the story of a movie, which is fine from time to time, so long as foveal vision is not our habitual mode of perception.

Once you acclimate to viewing the entire peripheral field of vision, spend the remaining time relaxing deeply into the experience and appreciating the feelings that arise while viewing peripherally. You might notice as a result of relaxing deeply into peripheral vision awareness that the sense of color, time, and space can become somewhat altered. We might even feel as if we are a little high.

Although these experiences can be pleasant for many people, they are not the main point of this meditation. Instead, the aim with this practice, or any TEM meditation, is to realize a greater sense of contextual awareness in our lives, so that our lives come into greater synchronization with the whole of reality.

Because we are almost constantly using our eyes throughout our active daily life, developing a second-nature awareness of the total visual field is incredibly helpful, for that broad awareness will make you highly conscious and keep you from being in a near constant, out-of-synch, beta wave state. As you practice, you will find that you are less stressed during the day and you are less perturbed by uncertainty. The more you practice, the more you will be buoyed from negative emotion. The power of conscious visual awareness should not be underestimated.

Chapter 7

Conscious Hearing

From the peripheral viewing exercise, you know that paying attention to the entire visual field can turn sight into a powerful portal of meditation. You might be surprised to discover that hearing can be used similarly.

What we think of as hearing actually works quite differently from how we might intuit the process. Sound waves enter the outer ear and travel through the ear canal to the eardrum, which vibrates from the sound waves. The vibrations affect three small bones in the middle ear, called the malleus, incus, and stapes.

The three bones amplify the sound vibrations and send them to the cochlea, a snail-shaped structure filled with fluid in the inner ear. Inside the cochlea, an elastic partition called the basilar membrane splits the cochlea into an upper and lower part. The basilar membrane is the foundation on which key hearing structures sit.

When vibrations inside the cochlea cause the fluid to ripple, a wave travels along the basilar membrane, where sensory hair cells on top of the basilar membrane are moved by the wave. The pitch of the sound is detected according to where the hair cells are on the membrane. The cells in the lower part of the cochlea detect higher-pitched sounds, whereas cells in the upper part of the snail-shaped cochlea detect lower-pitched sounds.

As the hair cells are moved by the wave, microscopic hairlike projections on top of the hair cells bump against the structure of the cochlea and bend, which causes channels at the tips of the hair cells to open up. Chemicals rush into the openings of the cells, which create electrical signals. The auditory nerve carries these signals to the brain. Upon receiving the electrical signals, the brain produces sound that we recognize from associated memories.

Essentially, what we think of as hearing is actually more like an illusion created by the brain when it is stimulated by electrical signals from the auditory nerve. Think about every movie that you have ever watched. All of the sound effects were probably produced by things other than what you see on the screen. For example, in old movies, horse footfalls might have been made by clacking together two dried coconut husk halves. Hearing the clacking, your brain just assumes that it is hearing a horse walking on asphalt. Even if you didn't know it was a horse movie and were unable to see any video, just hearing the coconut husks clacking together, your brain would probably conjure the image of a horse to fit the sound.

All senses rely on the brain filling in missing information with our memories of associated experience. Without the associated experience, we would be unable to make use of the information that the senses collect.

Conscious Hearing

With our refined understanding of the hearing process, we can begin to use the sense of hearing as a portal to meditation. For our meditative purposes, we will not rely on the illusory identification system that the brain uses to convey information to us. Instead, we will simply listen to all sound, without any attempt to identify or understand it.

We are going to open up our hearing by removing as much mental bias as possible. Because the human being has predator-like forward-facing eyes, and our ears are not mobile like those of many other animals, we are tuned to notice sound most acutely to the fore. Our ears are very poor at picking up sounds above, below, or behind the head. Based on the physical structure of our skulls and ears, our brains tend be inattentive in those sound-insensitive directions. So, for our exercise, we will intentionally listen equally in every direction, even if our ears can't pick up sound well in certain directions. We will also make no attempt to identify any particular sound that we hear, for that will lead us into a beta wave state, which is counter to meditation.

The process of conscious hearing is as follows:

Time

Two five-minute sessions.

Position

Sit or stand comfortably in a location where you will not be easily distracted.

Eyes

Eyes closed the first time that you practice and open the second time.

Process

Set your timer for five minutes, close your eyes, and relax the body as much as possible and listen carefully to all sound from all directions, near and far. Make no attempt to identify any sound. Instead, become engrossed in feeling sound. If you relax with this exercise, you will find that, in less than a minute, you are in a powerfully aware state of meditation.

If you find that you are attracted to or annoyed by any specific sound, your serial processing, noisy hemisphere is activated, and you are no longer in a meditative state. Thus, to remain in a meditative state, we simply accept all sounds without bias and without any attempt to identify them. Of course if there is a sound that is loud enough to damage the eardrum, then by all means, do what you can to protect your ears.

Once the timer goes off, start it again and redo the meditation, this time with your eyes open. At first, your attention might be tempted by the things in your visual field, but in that event, just keep returning your attention to the total auditory field. In short order, the mind will quiet, and you will find yourself in a vibrant state of meditation.

Final Thoughts on Conscious Hearing

The ear plays a vital role in our sense of balance. In the ear, just above the cochlea, are three small, fluid-filled loops called semicircular canals. Each of these loops detects a different type of movement: up-and-down, side-to-side, and tilting movements, respectively.

Each loop contains thousands of microscopic sensory hairs. When we move our heads, the fluid in the semicircular canals moves past the hairs, which causes them to bend. The bend creates an electrical signal that relays the type of movement that we are experiencing to our brain.

Also connected to the loops and the cochlea, two sacs convey information about how the head is moving in relation to gravity and acceleration. From these structures, we know when we are moving up or down in elevation and if we are standing or lying down.

Practicing conscious hearing over an extended period of time, you may find that your sense of balance and your movement quality, in general, improve. When I was teaching middle school in Japan, I had a terrible case of tinnitus, a ringing in the ears. Sometimes the ringing grew so loud that I could not hear what people were saying around me. Tinnitus is a disease for which the medical community has treatments that reduce symptoms, but for which they have no cure. Practicing the Warrior's Meditation combined with vagal breathing completely cured it within a few months.

Chapter 8

Conscious Olfaction

Olfaction, the sense of smell, is a highly underrated sense that we in the modern world tend to pay little conscious attention to. Of course for hunter-gatherers around the world, the sense of smell is considered a vital element for almost all activities of life.

In reality, the sense of smell is much more powerful than you might have realized. According to research from Rockefeller University that was published in the journal *Science*, the human nose can detect at least one trillion distinct scents. By comparison humans can discriminate among only several million different colors and just about half a million different audible tones (Bushdid et al.).

Modernized humans are quite out of touch with the sense of smell because we see little survival need for that sense in our highly insulated societies. Of course, as the Rockefeller University study showed, we have a much greater olfactory capacity than we have consciously realized, with much of the reaction to scents affecting our bodies in unconscious ways. As we do not have words for the trillion different scents that our noses can detect, we have no mental framework to consciously identify each smell. Still, our bodies are responding to those smells on many levels.

The sense of smell is a chemical detection sense, used to detect trace molecules in the environment, which is a capacity found even in single-celled organisms. For land mammals (including humans) the sense of smell works like this:

Molecules floating in the air land in the mucus at the roof of the nostrils and dissolve. Just under the mucus, specialized receptor cells (neurons) detect the odor. The neurons transmit the information via electrical signals to the back of the nose — specifically to the olfactory bulb, which is actually an extension of the brain. From there, the signals get sent directly to the limbic system, which influences emotions and memory, and to the neocortex, which affects conscious thought.

Have you ever noticed how certain smells can bring up vivid memories of people, places, and events from the distant past, even early childhood? The reason for this connection is that the sense of smell is essentially your memory and emotional center's direct link to the environment. The chemicals that touch your nose are, in effect, touching some of your brain's most developed, most ancient structures, ones that relate to emotion, memory, motivation, and automatic behaviors that are largely subconscious.

According the journal *Psychological Science*, human beings can even detect the smells of fear and disgust. When you detect those scents, your own brain responds unconsciously by registering the same emotions, which are actually discernible on your face. The research indicates that scents are, in a way, contagious (de Groot et al.).

Many people claim that women have a better sense of smell than do men, and that younger people tend to have a better sense of smell than do older people. Research experiments prove those statements to be true on average. The current theory as to why women have a better sense of smell than men on average is that women use the sense of smell to detect chemically suitable mates and to bond with their newborn infants.

Whether one may be male or female, young or old, the sense of smell is the single sense most connected to the part of our brain that regulates memory, emotion, and motivation — a part of the brain that is largely unconscious. Wouldn't it be a powerful thing if you were able to make some of that part of the brain more conscious, so that your memories, emotions, and motivations would be less reactive, less chaotic — and more harmonious and helpful to your life?

Conscious olfaction is going to help you do just that and more, for with conscious olfaction, you can toss out all the limitations that are typical of traditional meditation forms.

The process of conscious olfaction is as follows:

Time

Set your timer for fifteen minutes.

Position

Sit or stand as you please — just be comfortable.

Eyes

Eyes closed the first time that you practice and open the second time.

Process

Take full, smooth breaths with the intention of feeling the quality of the air as it travels through your nostrils, into the lungs, and back out again. Notice the general qualities of the air, such as the air pressure, the moisture, and freshness, as well as the overall sense of smell.

Do not get caught up in trying to identify any particular smell; just accept all smells while feeling the air traveling through the nasal passages.

Open your eyes to continue the meditation once you notice the shift to alpha, which is when your mind and body feel calm and relaxed.

What did you notice? Did your bodily feeling change? Did your body relax? Did your mind quiet?

Most people will find that they are noticeably calmed by simply becoming aware of smell. Generally speaking, when we stop paying attention to the sense of smell, it is easy to rapidly return to an unaware state. By maintaining awareness of smell for an extended period of time, the feeling of calm clarity grows deeper and deeper, lessening any habitual tendency to become anxious or depressed.

Your mind and body relax when smelling because you are consciously stimulating the limbic system, the emotional center of the brain.

Let me remind you that when smelling consciously, you intentionally contact an area of the brain that is normally inaccessible to your conscious mind, which means you have power to make beneficial changes in your brain related to emotions and past traumas. If when doing this meditation old negative emotions or mental narratives arise, the best way to reprogram the brain is to relax more into the process of conscious olfaction and sustain it until the negativity fades away. Just keep consciously smelling.

Another important point to note is that, once the shift to alpha occurs, when you open your eyes, you might notice that you are automatically peripherally aware, which demonstrates that you are in a conscious alpha state. If, when you open your eyes, you are not aware of the total visual field, it means that you did not yet make the shift to a conscious alpha state. In that case, close the eyes again and resume consciously noticing the sense of smell, bringing awareness into feeling the nasal passages and the lungs as you breathe until you relax still further, and then try opening the eyes again. Chances are you are now seeing the total visual field by default.

Note: you may find that your mind tries to identify specific smells with a narrative voice. When that is happening, it means that the serial processing mind is intruding, which can quickly take you out of meditation. Instead of getting caught up in labeling smells or fighting against that tendency, just calmly be aware that it is happening and then return to the awareness of all smells and the feeling of the nostrils as the air travels through them.

Do not in the least be concerned if you are unable to smell much, for your sense of smell may vary according to many factors, such as your physical health, age, the temperature, et cetera. What we are really aiming for is to get to the very essence of the sense of smell, which is actually feeling, for feeling is the true heart of awareness. With that in mind, if you have a poor sense of smell, simply pay attention to the feeling in your nostrils and air passages.

Many meditation traditions practice breath techniques, some of which can be quite elaborate. Virtually none of them couple breathing with attentiveness to smell, which, in my estimation, is a big oversight, for the sense of smell is vital to our psychological well-being.

Modern humans are highly addicted to using foveal (focused) vision, which stimulates an excitable, stressful, agitated state of mind from cortisol releases in the brain. A human being who is consciously attentive to smell is probably a very calm and clear individual.

One very simple approach to dealing with certain types of anxiety and depression is to become highly aware of the sense of smell and the feeling of breathing. Upon doing so, you may discover that you rapidly start feeling much better, as if you have been freed from a curse.

Final note: usually by the second time you practice conscious olfaction, you can do it easily with your eyes open from the outset.

Chapter 9

Conscious Tasting

The sense of taste, like that of smell, is a chemical detection sense, but unlike olfaction, which can detect more than a trillion different scents, the sense of taste is typically said to differentiate only among five different flavors — sweet, sour, salty, bitter, and savory, though some argue that pungency (spiciness) and the taste of fat are also sensed.

Taste works primarily in conjunction with the sense of smell to detect flavors. The tongue interacts with the texture of what is being masticated, which provides more information to the brain and affects the subjective feeling of taste. To get an idea of the relationship between taste and smell, plug your nose and try to taste something. You will note that the sense of taste is greatly limited when the sense of smell is impeded.

Taste allows humans to distinguish between nutritious and toxic foods. As digestive enzymes in saliva break down food into base chemicals, they are detected as flavors by the taste buds, which cover the tongue. The tongue has something between 2,000 and 5,000 taste buds. Still other taste buds are located in the throat, as well as on the roof and sides and at the back of the mouth. Each taste bud contains 50 to 100 taste receptor cells that transmit electrical signals to the brain, which then creates the taste that we experience.

The sense of taste is a mechanism that detects both nutrient and toxin. For example, sweetness typically indicates energy-rich foods, whereas bitterness warns of potential poisons.

As the taste buds are capable of detecting only a few distinct flavors, much of the sense of taste is affected by smell, which is powerfully affected by the temperature of the air and the food. When the food or the air where it is eaten is cold, the sense of smell will be impeded; and, thus, the sense of taste will be less acute. Warming food enhances our sense smell, which improves our ability to taste, which is why we prefer so many foods heated (and why ice cream is harder to taste overall).

Being aware that the sense of taste, like the sense of smell, is highly affected by temperature, we work with this sense during meditation with care not to be concerned about the specific tastes that we detect, for that will vary by temperature. Instead, pay attention to the overall sense, as well as the feeling of the tongue and the mouth in general.

The process of conscious taste is as follows:

Time

Set your timer for fifteen minutes.

Position

Sit or stand as you please — just be comfortable.

Eyes

Eyes closed the first time you try it.

Process

Become vibrantly aware of the feeling in the mouth, as well as the general sense of taste.

You may detect traces of flavors that you consumed earlier in the day, but make no attempt to identify specific tastes. Just be aware of the sense of taste and the feeling in the mouth as if it were your first time ever experiencing the mouth.

Be careful to notice when the shift to alpha occurs.

As you can see, the process is very simple. And, for most people, just paying attention to the sense of taste and the feeling in the mouth is sufficient to make a shift to alpha wave within a minute.

Final Thoughts on Conscious Tasting

Much of the time, when we eat, we are not paying attention to our senses, so we are getting only a surface-level enjoyment of the eating process. Because we are not being attentive, we tend to eat quickly, and that leads to overeating because we do not notice that we are full until we have already eaten beyond a healthful amount. Slowing down the eating process so that you can be attentive to your senses while eating can help to curb the tendency to overeat. Slowing down will also allow you to enjoy eating more and stop taking food for granted.

Chapter 10

Conscious Feeling

Conscious feeling is first and foremost about bodily awareness. Such awareness includes attention to proprioception and interoception. Proprioception is the sense of where the body is in space. It is like an internal map that tells you where your body parts are without having to look at them. Interoception is the sense of the physiological condition of the body. Interoception gives us information about sensual touch, warmth, coolness, muscular activity, pain, tickle, itch, hunger, thirst, the need to yawn or take a breath, sexual arousal, heartbeat, vasomotor activity, and fullness of the bladder, stomach, rectum, and esophagus.

Our bodily awareness is also informed by receptors in our joints, muscles, ligaments, and connective tissue, which give information on compression and decompression of the joints. This information travels through the spinal cord and into unconscious parts of the brain. Because much of this information is unconscious, unless you actively intend to notice your body, you are likely to be unaware of your bodily position.

Even though you are not always consciously aware of your body's position, your body is generally able to keep you upright and safe through the various activities of your day, which is why I refer to it as a generally unconscious sense.

By bodily awareness, I am not referring to thoughts or opinions about your appearance, but instead to the direct sensory awareness of your body's condition, feeling, and position. I include with bodily awareness the feeling of your body's contact with the environment, which could include the feeling of the floor beneath your feet, the feeling of your butt against the chair, the feeling of your skin touching clothing, the air, et cetera — the entire internal and external cacophony of bodily sensations.

Medical and psychological literature describes heightened body awareness as leading to worsening symptoms of anxiety and panic disorders, and to an increase in pain. The reason for this outcome is that the medical and psychological community has defined *awareness* as being focus. When we focus on physical symptoms, we may ruminate on and experience magnification symptoms, leading us to states of high anxiety.

This medical/psychological idea of bodily awareness is fundamentally different from what body-mind practitioners mean by awareness. Body-mind practitioners derive their idea of awareness from a relaxed perception, not an anxious perception.

Many body-mind modalities aim to enhance bodily awareness, among which tai chi, yoga, Feldenkrais, Alexander technique, and breathwork are popular options, but we could look to traditional meditation as an exemplar of the relaxed body-mind approach.

In traditional forms of meditation, one focuses to exclusion while relaxing. Because body-mind modalities use relaxed concentration, the resulting awareness is coming from an alpha brainwave state, which leads to positive medical and psychological outcomes. A tense or anxious focus on feelings would reflect a beta wave state that leads to increased anxiety and the tendency for negative outcomes noted by the medical community.

In fact, numerous studies demonstrate the benefits of a relaxed awareness of the bodily state. These studies suggest that bodily awareness, as it is used in body-mind practices, may help to alleviate diseases such as chronic lower back pain (Mehling et al.), congestive heart failure (Baas et al.), chronic renal failure (Christensen et al.), and irritable bowel syndrome (Eriksson et al.).

Because of our understanding of the awareness paradox (Chapter 5), the Total Embodiment Method takes awareness a step further than the traditional body-mind approach. Instead of relaxed concentration on a specific point of the body, we relax into awareness of the entire body.

Counterintuitively, a relaxed total awareness makes us remarkably sensitive to subtle bodily cues, without creating anxiety, much like the way we can see the subtle blinking of dim stars better when we are attentive to peripheral vision.

Here is the TEM process of conscious bodily awareness:

Time

Allow about a minute between each step. The total time for the entire sequence need not take more than fifteen minutes for your initial experience.

Position

At first, simply be comfortable in a place without too many distractions. If you have a tendency to fall asleep or become drowsy when lying down, you may want to sit upright or stand instead.

Eyes

Open or closed, as you like.

Process

We're going to break the body up into sections at first to ease our way into the process of bodily awareness. Please note that this sectional approach is only temporary. We will soon transition into full bodily awareness as our default practice.

As you do this exercise, your attention may be drawn to focus on particular points of discomfort or pain. Instead of focusing on those specific points, simply return your attention to the total space that you are working on according to the steps below, allowing the painful or uncomfortable points to be in the background of your awareness.

Sit comfortably while paying vibrant attention to the whole of your feet and consciously relax them.

Next, vibrantly feel the area between your ankles and your knees and consciously relax those areas.

Now, feel the space from your knees to your hips and consciously relax that area.

When you are ready, vibrantly feel the area from your hips to your lower ribcage and relax it.

Next, give your attention to the area between your lower ribs and your collar bones and relax the area.

When you feel ready for the next step, pay vibrant attention to the area between your collar bones and the top of your head. Relax it deeply.

Now, feel the space between your collar bones and your elbows. Consciously relax that space.

Next, notice the area between your elbows and your wrists. Relax.

Now, feel your hands and fingers. Especially relax this area.

Finally, pay attention to the total space of your entire body, the inner dimension as well as the surface area, and relax the entire body such that there is just enough tension to remain upright.

Final Thoughts on Conscious Feeling

You might notice that paying attention to and relaxing the body's areas outlined above seems to create a feeling of lightness in those areas. You might also notice that paying attention to the entire body rapidly takes you into a conscious alpha wave state. Conversely, focusing your mind on a specific point of pain or discomfort is almost guaranteed to cause the mind to shift into beta wave, which will only cause more pain and discomfort.

Beta wave states should not be associated with awareness, for that ungrounded state lacks context. Feeling with contextual awareness, through alpha wave, improves circulation, reduces inflammation, and relaxes the entire nervous system, so that the body can begin to recover.

A last note on bodily awareness: people tend to associate awareness with tension, because we are told to pay attention exclusively (beta wave) so many times as children in school, for example. Paying attention in the way we were taught in school puts us in a state of tension. Because of the long-held confusion between awareness and attention, which is actually *at-tension*, it may take some practice to teach the brain how to relax out of the beta wave habit and into awareness.

Yes, it is possible to be aware of the entire body while being mentally tense, but that approach will tend not to lead to positive health outcomes, because it will rapidly drain the body of energy. For the healing process to work, relaxation and conservation of energy are vital, which is why most of our bodies' recovery processes happen while we sleep. The secret to feeling and healing is to learn to relax into the process, so that your brain is not consuming so much energy.

Chapter 11

Final Thoughts on the Senses

You might note that the scientific description of each sense ends with statements like "the electrical signals travel to the brain, which then creates the sensation that you experience." What these statements really mean, if the theory is correct, is that the brain in effect imagines reality based upon associated memories. The scientific literature could just as accurately have written, "the electric signals travel to the brain, where some great mystery of consciousness occurs that we do not yet understand."

Acknowledging that most of what we perceive of the world may be a creation of the brain (or its projection) can be very helpful to the meditative process, because we can begin to shift our mindset away from the ideas that the world is merely around us, and that it is dead matter. If we view the world as dead matter, we tend to lose respect for it, for our environment, for our bodies. The materialistic view tends to deaden awareness, and that runs contrary to the process of meditation.

Once you realize that, at least to a great degree, what you perceive may be occurring only within your brain, you can then begin to look at what your brain is perceiving/projecting with great curiosity, with fresh eyes, as it were, not assuming that what you perceive of the world or of yourself is ultimately true.

At the very heart of meditation lies the ability to continually refresh awareness, so that our perception can be free of the many conceptual traps of the mind. The result of that process is that you can be, as directly as possible, in touch with the moment, as it presents itself, and less captivated by the ruminations of the mind.

Although our brains may be in truth creating our sense of reality based entirely upon electric signals and associated memories, we should still pay very close attention to everything that we perceive, for in the nature of awareness, you will find the transformative value of meditation. What awareness shows you specifically is far less important than the fact that our brains are fully engaging in the awareness game that is meditation.

The trick, once we start playing the game of awareness, is not to stop. Play with awareness in every moment you can. The more that you play the game, the easier it will be for the brain to sustain awareness, for the brain learns over time to enable greater access to awareness.

Now that we have experienced consciously shifting to alpha wave through the portals of each sense, we can take the awareness game a step further by combining the senses to create a harmonic effect. A harmonic effect is an effect that is greater than the sum of its parts. Take humming and whistling, for example: each of these sounds, when produced separately, creates a specific energetic effect, but when combined, they create an entirely new energetic effect that transcends both humming and whistling.

For an example of the harmonic effect, visit
https://richardlhaight.com/harmonic

Let's level up our game!

Part III

Basic TEM Practice

Natural is a much misconstrued word, for in truth, everything within the universe is by definition natural. So, with that in mind, when I use the term natural, I am referring to the instinctive qualities that would emerge within human beings if raised in an environment that supported contextual sensory awareness, like that of a hunter-gatherer: the situation that human beings have been in until just the last few thousand years at most. You may be surprised to hear that people still live under the "natural" pressures of hand-to-mouth survival as hunter-gatherers in various places on the planet.

People in modern civilization tend to think we have it far better than the hunter-gatherers, but I suggest that our modern lifestyles have certain disadvantages that have largely gone unnoticed. We tend to have a much higher prevalence of psychological disorder than do hunter-gatherers. Our bodies are, in general, far less suited to handle the rigors of living in the natural world, because we hyperinsulate our houses and because we tend to eat too much and too often. Believe it or not, there are certain health advantages to being spatially aware, fasting, and being regularly exposed to environmental stressors such as extremes in temperature. In a lot of ways, our minds and our bodies are suffering from too much focus, too much mental stress, and not enough environmental pressure to ground our awareness and fortify our bodies.

Because life in modern civilization is so easy, far more of us die from diseases related to obesity than we do from starvation. In fact, dying of starvation in the modern world is almost unheard of, and that is a wonderful blessing. But, considering our circumstances, if we want to live a vibrant, healthy life, we can begin learning the simple healthy lessons that the natural lifestyle of hunter-gatherers has to offer, including the benefits of using the senses consciously, bodily awareness, fasting, and acclimating the body to weather extremes.

Don't get me wrong: I am not saying that the hunter-gatherer lifestyle is better. I have spent time with hunter-gatherers, who were headhunters only 30 years ago. Some of the tribal people whom I met and stayed with surely took heads during their lives. Let's not idealize anyone. But, being honest, they have certain areas of wisdom, just as do we. We should learn all the wisdom we can from anyone who has it to offer.

In many ways, Samurai and hunter-gatherers had a lot in common, which is probably why I felt so close to the hunter-gatherers whom I have met. Samurai, like hunter-gatherers, knew how important it was to be fully aware and physically healthy at all times. They did not have an insurance policy to cover them if they made a mistake, nor did they have an emergency room around the corner in the event of an accident.

Many of us in the modern world take our health for granted because we know that we have a safety net. Of course, not everyone has a perfect fallback, but all of us in modern civilization have a greater safety net than do the hunter-gatherers of the world. Simply knowing that we have that protection can lull us into a state of inattentive carelessness. An example of our lulled state can be readily seen in the careless actions of campers, who will break sticks for the camp fire over their knees. You would never see a hunter-gatherer break sticks with their bodies for any reason because they know it can result in a disabling injury. If your survival is dependent upon you being able to walk for miles each day to get food and supplies, even a small injury can put your life in danger and weaken your tribe's chances of survival. Care and awareness are essential to both survival and a healthy brain, so we are wise to proceed as if we don't have a safety net.

The TEM approach takes the best wisdom of the Samurai and the hunter-gatherers and seeks to employ it in our daily lives, so that we can become more vibrantly aware and healthy, while still potentially having the safety nets of society.

As you practice TEM, please bear in mind that it is meant to blend with your daily life, while challenging you to be more aware on all levels. TEM is meant to challenge your brain so that it becomes more flexible, aware, and in tune with life in the moment. Your brain is your most important tool. You would be wise to keep it vibrantly healthy.

In Part III, we add one additional step, spherical awareness, to the sensory portals of meditation that you learned in Part II. By combining these portals, a synergy will emerge that is greater than the sum of its parts. The steps combined make up the Warrior's Meditation, which is the basic TEM practice method.

Once we explore the Warrior's Meditation, we will learn the proper mindset of meditation, how to deal with mental resistance, and how to become ever more flexible with the practice, so that we can begin to integrate TEM more thoroughly into our active daily lives.

Chapter 12

Spherical Awareness

As I state in this book's introduction, Osaki Sensei and I did not use the five sensory portals as our means of meditation when we trained together. The five senses were the means by which I meditated before joining Osaki Sensei's dojo. Because of the intensive bodily awareness that we had already achieved through our martial arts training, we needed no help getting to the level of meditation that I describe here as spherical awareness. I incorporated the senses into the meditation process as a means of lifting up beginners to the stage of meditation that Osaki Sensei and I were working with in Japan.

Spherical awareness training is extremely useful for martial, healing, and meditation arts. The method is unique. I had never heard of any method like it before our discovery of it. That stated, based on what I have since been told by masters of certain other traditions, I am almost certain that I am not the first to have discovered it, though I may be one of the first ever to codify the method. Here is how we came upon this training technique.

We began uncovering this training method by way of practicing sotai-ho on each other. Sotai-ho is the Japanese therapeutic art that I was licensed to practice. Through our explorations of sotai-ho, we noticed a certain light, full feeling in the body. Once we became sufficiently aware of this feeling, we sought to achieve it purely through meditation.

We discovered that we could use the heightened awareness to search our own bodies for heavy-feeling places and, merely by lightly intending toward that spot, we found that our bodies would begin to move on their own as they stretched out and opened the formerly heavy area. At first we were really surprised and spooked by the experience.

After the experience, I began researching the nervous system in hopes of discovering what might be happening, and I was relieved to discover that there was a scientific explanation for the phenomenon. I was pleased to discover that the automatic movement was a result of a highly stimulated vagus nerve that triggered an autonomic nervous system response, specifically in the parasympathetic nervous system, which can cause unconscious movement that stimulates recovery and healing in the body.

When we hear that someone's body moved unconsciously, we tend to think of it as quite spooky or dubious, but all of us have experienced unconscious parasympathetic movement. We tend to overlook its oddness thanks to the commonality of its occurrence. Yawning is a perfect example of unconscious parasympathetic movement.

Yawning is a parasympathetic nervous system response to stress or tiredness. The movement, stretching, and breathing that are stimulated by a yawn are not consciously controlled by us, though we are aware that it is happening at the time. Yawning helps to relax the body to bring the system toward balance.

What Osaki Sensei and I were experiencing was a highly vigorous version of yawning which took on unexpected dimensions that brought about a body balancing effect, reduced inflammation, and greatly heightened relaxed awareness. What I teach now as vagal breathing is a basic way for beginners to tap into some of those effects.

Although the therapeutic effects of the meditative awareness we tapped into were tremendously inspiring, the real eye-opener was how it affected our martial arts training. Along with many other beneficial effects, I found that my ability to execute techniques skyrocketed. Recognizing my improvement, Osaki Sensei began introducing me to advanced skills in the sword, staff, and open-hand, using the feeling that we had discovered from our therapy and meditation explorations as the engine for our movement.

With our new approach, we found that every aspect of my ability improved dramatically, and within a few years I was given master's licenses in the four Samurai arts that Sensei had taught at that time. Sensei honored me with the tremendous responsibility to teach these ancient traditions by using our newfound approach. Please allow me to share it with you.

Spherical Awareness Exercise

Imagine a light, pleasant feeling in your chest. Once you get a sense for the feeling, spread it throughout your body. If you find there are areas of the body that seem resistant to this light feeling, you are getting an experience of what I describe earlier in this chapter as heavy areas in my body. Do not try to force those areas to lighten at this time. Just take note of them without focusing on them.

Next, imagine that light, pleasant feeling spreading beyond your body spherically to create a positive atmosphere in the space around you. Be sure that your feeling does not stop at surfaces, but moves right through them. Walls, floors, and ceilings need not limit your intention or awareness, so softly extend your feeling/intention beyond those things.

Doing this simple exercise will subtly — or not so subtly — change your posture and breathing in healthy ways, for your vagus nerve will be highly responsive. These beneficial changes will affect your blood pressure, heart rate, digestive processes, mental states, and ... everything, really. People and animals around you will unconsciously respond to you differently when you are spherically aware in this way.

What Osaki Sensei and I discovered in our practice was that relaxation is the key to gaining many of the positive effects of this exercise. Putting too much tension into this process will rapidly tire the body and brain, so do not try to force your feeling out, beyond the body. Instead, enjoy the process as if you were an angel stretching its wings. Allow your feeling to be free of the limits of your body, but do not try to escape the body. Instead, allow feeling to extend from the very core of the body toward the rest of the world.

Of course, do not expect that you will physically feel the objects that your intention is moving through, for that is not likely to happen. Instead, just enjoy the feeling of the light, spacious awareness that this exercise brings to your life.

One of the challenges that can make this exercise difficult is our developed sense of proprioception, which is our awareness of where our body is in space. Proprioception tells you not only where you are, but it also tells you where your body stops. Of course, this sense is vital for survival, so you are less likely to walk off a cliff, for example. There is a disadvantage to unconscious proprioception, which is that it can create a powerful sense that you are separate from everything around you, which even science would tell you is not the case.

Every atom consists of particles, some of which are electrically charged. What you feel as physical touch is actually the resistance of the nuclei in your atoms when they come in proximity to the nuclei of other atoms. The nuclei never actually touch. No atomic nucleus in your body has ever actually touched another, but the forces within the atoms that attract and resist each other create what we experience as touch and distance. You are actually feeling the forces of atoms, which is interpreted by your brain as physicality.

Using the idea of energy fields as our model, we can just imagine our energy field as being a positive, healthy force that extends outward to the benefit of everything around us.

Dealing with Fear

Certain individuals may experience visceral fear when they practice spherical awareness. Such fear is indicative of a traumatized nervous system, usually a result of being taken advantage of in a way that made us want to shell ourselves off for protection. Thus, victims of rape, or of emotional or physical abuse, might be prone to fear the spherical awareness exercise because they have unconsciously pulled their energies inward. The tendency to pull inward starts with a desire to hide from the world and indicates a nervous system that is stuck in prey mode.

The problem with being stuck in prey mode is that it actually attracts predators, who are constantly seeking weak-energy individuals to prey on. Pulling into ourselves produces a very weak energy that shows in our posture, our emotions, our actions and reactions every moment of our lives. Being stuck in prey mode is like holding a neon sign above your head that reads, "I'm a target." Narcissistic and sociopathic individuals are especially adept at reading that sign.

Of course, when we were originally traumatized, we probably had no better option than to pull into ourselves. But now that you are practicing spherical awareness, you have a means not only of healing the trauma, but also of pulling your nervous system out of prey mode, so that you can start to fully interact with life again.

Many teachings might say that you should not open up your energies, but those teachings really refer to emotional energies, not awareness. If you are highly emotional, of course, that can put you in danger. Emotions have their place, but we should be judicious about whom we share them with. Awareness, in contrast, is a quality that a predator fears in potential targets.

Think of every person whom you highly respect in the world. Chances are those people feel large to you, energetically speaking. They stand tall and express themselves authentically. They seem wise but fearless, which is probably why you respect them. Nature respects awareness, and it crushes weakness.

Energetic weakness must not be confused with relaxation, for energetic weakness is actually indicative of a highly anxious state. Likewise, energetic hardness does not equate to strength, for energetic hardness is just another form of insecurity trying to disguise itself by wearing a strong mask. Relaxed awareness brings the balance that we seek.

Final thoughts on Spherical Awareness

The spherical awareness exercise is well worth practicing, but if you find any difficulty with it, spend some extra time practicing the sensory portals that we explored in the previous chapters, so that the brain becomes ever more flexible. As the brain increases in flexibility and awareness, spherical awareness will become easier to achieve and will require less and less effort. A hallmark of a master Samurai was that he was always spherically aware. With practice you will get there.

Lastly, there are many, many ways to modify this method. What I have shared here is but one of nearly infinite possibilities. Regardless of which one you practice, the key to success is the same — extend awareness equally in every direction from the core of your body. Because the human senses tend to project forward, our brains are somewhat dull in awareness above, below, and to the sides of our bodies. Although those directions are weak, we are weakest in awareness directly behind our bodies.

Being mindful of the weaknesses of our awareness, we are wise to devote a little extra attention to those weaker directions to create a more balanced brain.

Chapter 13

The Warrior's Meditation

The Warrior's Meditation is the basic level 1 TEM meditation practice. It establishes a neural foundation that will eventually allow awareness to seep into your active daily life. Much like the master Samurai, who finds tremendous calm clarity even in the chaos of battle, with practice, you too can find calm clarity in your active, daily life.

To get a mental picture of the Warrior's Meditation, imagine a battlefield scenario with a single Samurai surrounded by multiple opponents intent on killing him. A novice's attention jumps from opponent to opponent in an anxious attempt to defend himself. He will soon tire and be defeated. An expert warrior spreads his attention evenly in all directions but still experiences anxiety as he mentally plans his tactics. His thoughts and anxiety may be his downfall if his opponents are truly skilled. A master's attention, like the expert's, is spread evenly, but he is as calm as a still pond. With no thought of what his actions might be, his body takes the right action according to the requirements of the moment.

You may wonder how the Samurai's experience bears any resemblance to your modern life. Ideally, no armies or assassins are trying to attack you or your town.

In one way, we modern people are not so different from the Samurai. With our busy lives, we don't have time to spend hours a day in meditation. Instead, we need a meditation that blends with our high-pressure, fast-paced lives, right here, right now, so that the doing flows from a depth of awareness; the ability to express from a depth of awareness is exactly what the Warrior's Meditation is intended to help you do.

Because reading is almost certain to keep a person new to the TEM process locked in beta wave, I suggest, before trying the Warrior's Meditation, that you read through the meditation steps to familiarize yourself with the process, so that when you try the meditation, you do not have to read. After you have familiarized yourself with the steps of the Warrior's Meditation, set the book down and try it.

Note: we will be using the senses as a portal into meditation, so in the event that you are missing any of the five primary senses, have no concern, as the brain will compensate for what is absent. For example, if you are deaf, during the phase in which we are paying attention to the auditory sense, you could simply pay attention to the feeling of your ears. Thus, you will end up at the same place as anyone with all five senses.

Time

Generally speaking, your first experience with the Warrior's Meditation will take between 15 and 20 minutes. The time will vary from person to person because feeling your way through the process is vital. After you're comfortable with the steps and have experienced the Warrior's Meditation a few times, setting a timer for a duration of your choosing is good, so that you don't have to think about time during dedicated practice sessions.

Position

Just be comfortable. I do not recommend lying down initially, as you may become drowsy and drift off to sleep. Once your body gains an association between meditation and sleep, it will be extremely difficult to stay alert during meditation.

Eyes

Open for basic practice.

Process

Begin the Warrior's Meditation by doing several vagal breaths, which will rapidly relax the body and mind. Here is a summary of the vagal breathing process described in Chapter 3:

- Take in a full breath and use the breath to stretch the lungs in ways that feel really good. You can use the abdomen, spine, shoulders, and neck to alter the stretching pressure. Make it feel wonderful. Exhale slowly. Repeat. Visit www.richardlhaight.com/vagal to see a demonstration of vagal breathing.
- Once your body and mind feel calm and clear, move on to the next step in the meditation

Gaze straight ahead, taking in the entirety of the visual field, just as we did during the peripheral viewing exercise in Chapter 6. You can use your extended arms to find the outer edge of your peripheral vision if you are having trouble getting out of focused vision.

The way to find the peripheral edge is to gaze straight ahead and without moving your eyes, extend your arms directly out to your sides. Move the hands back just far enough that you can't see them, then begin wiggling your fingers. Slowly move the hands forward until the wiggling motion is barely detectable by your peripheral vision. Now, while keeping the wiggling fingers at the very edge of the visual field, move them circularly in a clockwise motion to find the entire outer edge of the peripheral field.

What you will find is that the edge of our peripheral vision is vertically narrow, with only about a 90 degree range, and horizontally wide, with about 180 degrees of visibility. Once you have found the entire outer edge of the peripheral field of vision, relax your arms.

We don't want any straining during this meditation, so be sure to spend several minutes relaxing into peripheral vision to acclimate to it and allow your perception to open up before moving to the next step. Once you have acclimated and relaxed into awareness of the total visual field, move to the next step.

Become aware of the entire audible field by allowing all sound to come into the body without focusing on or trying to identify any particular sound. If we set aside our biases, likes and dislikes, we will find that we can do this meditation even in a noisy space because all sound will be acceptable. That said, to protect your ears, it is always wise to avoid exposing them to extremely loud sounds. Spend a few minutes applying vibrant awareness to all sounds near and far. Once you are able to relax into conscious hearing, move to the next step.

Become aware of the sense of smell and the feeling of air traveling through the nostrils and into the lungs. Although you may notice smells of the location you are in, the smell of your own body, and the smell of food eaten earlier in the day, do not attempt to identify them. Just notice the entire cacophony of smells without allowing your attention to be caught by specific smells. If you are unable to detect any smells, have no concern, as noticing particular smells is not the aim. Instead, open up feeling in an unbiased way without concern for the details. Relax and enjoy.

Direct your awareness to the sense of taste and the feeling within the mouth. You might notice the taste of some the things that you ate earlier in the day, but do not take interest in identifying those specific tastes. Just enjoy exploring the general sense of taste and the sensations of the mouth, such as warmth, moisture, hardness, softness, et cetera. Finding a balance between relaxation and vibrant engagement is vital here. Give yourself a few minutes to acclimate to the sense of taste before moving to the next step in the meditation, bodily awareness.

Become aware of the entire surface area of the body, as well as the inner sensations of your body as if you were experiencing it for the very first time. There may be points of discomfort or pain, but be careful not to allow your mind to focus on those points to exclusion. Instead, allow awareness to grace the entirety of the body simultaneously. Give yourself a little time to relax into total awareness of the body.

Finally, allow your meditative feeling to stretch beyond the body into the surrounding space spherically. You could imagine it as if the very essence of your being were unleashed to feel the space beyond the confines of the body.

The temptation for many people at this stage is to start creating a lot of inner pressure in the unconscious attempt to blow one's self up like a balloon, but that approach runs counter to our aim of finding a relaxed awareness that can aid us in daily life. Instead of becoming willful, this process should be enjoyable and liberating.

If you are in a room, your intention and feeling will tend to unconsciously stop at surfaces by habit. As intention can extend beyond surfaces, the tendency for feeling to stop at surfaces is indicative of a limiting belief. There is no reason to believe that surfaces have any power over intention, so let intention and feeling flow beyond the walls, ceiling, and floor.

Remain unconditionally aware in this way for the remainder of your meditation time, with the intent of using less and less focus as you proceed. Relax and enjoy the fullness of being.

One of the many benefits of this final stage of the Warrior's Meditation is that we become more functionally attentive to the total space around us. This profoundly benefits the brain as it starts to change to allow for a more contextual awareness of the world around us, as well as a deeper, more contextual awareness of what is happening within the psyche.

Rising from the Warrior's Meditation

The goal of the Warrior's Meditation is not to be sedentary, although it can certainly be used for deep, sedentary meditation. Ultimately, the goal is to incorporate contextual awareness into our active daily lives. Be careful not to associate rising to your feet or standing with the end of meditation, as it would be in many other meditative traditions. Instead, we want to maintain vibrant spatial awareness as we rise to a standing position, as we walk around, and as we go about our daily life.

Generally speaking, practicing the Warrior's Meditation does not lower blood-pressure so much that we need to worry about fainting as we attempt to stand. Just to be safe, though, it is wise to get the blood-pressure up a bit before standing. We can use this precaution as an opportunity to practice remaining in a meditative state while moving to raise our blood pressure.

The solution is to remain spherically aware while doing the movement that is meant to elevate your blood-pressure. We can use the idea of the windows on your computer screen as a good analogy for what we are going to do here. With your computer, you are able to place a window in the foreground and another window in the background. Similarly, we will keep spatial awareness in the foreground while allowing the stimulating movement to be in the background of awareness. In this way, the movement will be incorporated into your meditation and will not take you out of it. Shift your body weight left and right, forward and backward, and wiggle your fingers and toes a bit. Doing those simple movements should be sufficient to elevate your blood-pressure to safe levels before you rise to a standing position.

Now that you are up, see how long you can maintain spatial awareness as you go about your day.

Summary of the Warrior's Meditation

1. Take several vagal breaths to relax the body and mind
2. Pay attention to the total visual field
3. Notice all sound near and far

4. Notice the sense of smell and the feeling in the breathing passages
5. Notice the sense of taste and the feeling in the mouth
6. Notice the feeling of the entire body
7. Expand your feeling spherically beyond the body to the space around you
8. Rise by keeping special awareness primary in your attention, move your fingers and toes, and lean left and right to be sure your blood pressure is at a safe level before you stand. Stand in awareness.

Refining the Process

If we find ourselves getting a little stressed by the sensory process of the Warrior's Meditation, we might be straining a little too much with the senses. The most common strain is with the eyes, when they unconsciously bulge in the attempt to see the peripheral field. The solution is to soften the eyes, allowing them to see the peripheral field without strain. While relaxing the eyes, it is also a good idea to relax the shoulders, a common place where we hold unconscious tension.

Another common way in which we stress our bodies during this meditation is when we try to hold onto all the senses simultaneously. To resolve this issue, as we move from sight to sound to smell, et cetera, just relax and trust that the previous senses will inform us as necessary without our trying to attend to all senses simultaneously.

At some point the senses will start informing you without effort on your part. I first noticed this effect when I fell asleep on the grass at a park in Japan. It was a beautiful warm spring day, and I was feeling just about as cozy as could be. I fell asleep during meditation only to wake up to a powerful inner warning as I felt an ominous pressure bearing down on me from behind. I shot out of sleep and turned my head to look toward the pressure. Sure enough there was a strange man walking right up behind me staring right at me.

Considering where I was lying and the lay of the land, his approach was clearly a conscious invasion of my space, for I was well off the walking path but clearly visible from it. I have no idea what his intentions were, but I doubt they were good.

As soon as our eyes made contact, he turned abruptly and moved away. I wondered how I knew someone was stalking toward me, as I was asleep and didn't consciously hear anything. Expanded relaxation allowed me to escape a possible attack. Over time, you will develop trust in the meditation and in the senses to inform you when necessary. Functional trust comes with much practice and experience. Let us practice our meditation process with trust.

Final Thoughts on the Warrior's Meditation

As I indicated in the Introduction, meditation provides us with many scientifically verified physical and mental health benefits. With regular practice of the Warrior's Meditation, you will discover a number of powerful benefits.

Regular meditation can create a feeling of growing expansiveness, which seems to psychologically buoy meditators and make them less reactive to stressors and what we might have formerly perceived as personal attacks. Practicing meditation also helps the meditator to see the self in a nonpersonal way, which allows for a tremendous objectivity and insight and can serve to liberate us from unhealthy emotional patterns. This nonpersonalizing effect slowly inoculates us against pettiness, selfishness, neuroses, and narcissism.

You will begin to notice that, more and more, inner and outer negativity seems to flow past you without sticking. As you become less reactive to things that are unworthy of your attention, you will find that you are spared from a lot of wasted time and energy.

You might also notice through the practice of the Warrior's Meditation that your body seems to awaken, which allows it to move independently to evade unseen dangers or go ahead in beneficial directions. I, for example, allow all of my writing to be done by the body in this way. In effect, it seems as if the book is being written through my body, rather than that I am writing it. I am sure that many musicians and athletes have had similar experiences from time to time. The state is flowing and can sometimes be referred to as being "in the zone."

I'm sure with practice, many, if not all, of these benefits will be realized by you, but don't fool yourself, for it will take daily practice. That brings us to neuroplasticity.

The brain is the most fluid organ of your body. It actually changes with every experience that we have, for that is how the brain helps us to adapt to our environment. The adaptability of the brain is called neuroplasticity.

Neuroplasticity is the brain's ability to continuously change throughout the life of an individual. The primary changes occur as we sleep. During sleep the brain re-allocates resources from less used neural pathways to ones that have been more used throughout the day. The ability of the brain to change through neuroplasticity is extremely empowering for individuals who make use of that ability.

As stated at the beginning of this book, numerous studies have shown a link between meditation practice and changes in cortical thickness of the brain, as well as changes in regional brain activity associated with fear, anger, depression, anxiety, and attention. These studies also show improvements in the body's abilities to heal itself (Sasmita et al.). It appears that these changes are a result of structural alterations in the brain as a result of neuroplasticity (Kong et al.).

If you skip days in your practice, you are losing the opportunity for positive brain restructuring through neuroplasticity when you sleep, for the meditation-stimulated changes can occur only if you have challenged your brain with meditation that day. Ten to fifteen minutes per day is a great start. If ten to fifteen minutes per day is not possible, then do five minutes per day, but don't skip days, for you will soon find that you fall out of the meditation pattern and back into the old unconscious patterns.

Q&A

The meditation technique that you teach is very similar to the teaching of Vipassana meditation, except for one detail: the direction of observation. In Vipassana meditation, observations are directed inwards, whereas the direction of observation with the Warrior's Meditation seems to be outward, to the world. Do you think that I can practice both of these meditations, or should I only do one? Both require you to eventually live permanently in the mode of meditation.

As we practice the meditations found in this book, the illusion of separation between inner and outer dimensions begins to fade, which is to say that insight and "outsight" become one and the same — you are the world; the world is you. Once we have that realization, the question of where to direct observation will become meaningless, for observation is no longer exclusive.

With regard to Vipassana, if it does eventually lead to continual living meditation in some of its practitioners, then the proper practice of it must eventually dissolve the unhelpful illusions of separation.

As for which meditation is best for you to practice, in my experience, experimentation is highly rewarding, so it might be a great idea for you to play with both and see what comes of the search, if you feel so inclined.

The experimental approach to meditation is most effective if it is done very thoroughly, with the realization that our perceptions and capacities deepen and refine as we go, so what might have seemed ineffective in early experimentation could become effective later on. While training with my teacher in Japan, I would retest my experiments from time to time and was greatly rewarded for the effort. If we experiment with curiosity and joy, the awakening process will be an adventure!

During meditation I keep having the thought that I'm not doing it right. You have said that is a normal feeling early on, but I still have it, even after practicing for some months.

The feeling that you are doing it wrong is probably coming from an insecurity that may manifest as perfectionism. Perfectionism comes from the serial processing hemisphere and represents as a beta wave state, which means it is counter to the meditative process.

Perfectionism is born of an egoic idea that we should be flawless at what we are doing, which is impossible. Fundamentally, the feeling comes from seeking approval or avoiding responsibility. If we feel we can be the best at something, perfectionism might goad us forward and produce great results with skills and knowledge, but because perfectionism is an unconscious energy, it is opposed to awareness. What will happen if we feed perfectionism is that we will eventually give up in areas where we judge ourselves to be insufficient. As human beings we have many areas that are out of balance, so perfectionism will cause us to polarize our abilities. We will shine in some areas and decay in others because of deep-seated insecurities.

Some degree of insecurity is perfectly normal, and it is also probably true that you are not doing the meditations perfectly. The trick is to simply not believe the inner narratives and instead continue bumbling your way through the meditation process. As you move forward, however clumsily, you will gradually gain awareness, and your practice will naturally refine itself.

The brain needs time and exposure to acclimate. At this early stage of the meditation process, we can look upon meditation much like learning to ride a bicycle. We're going to lose balance a lot early on, but eventually, if we persist, we'll be able to ride with no hands.

With persistent practice, we reduce effort and find so much clarity that there will no longer be a sense of self to make a mistake, and once we have that experience we will realize that "I" can never do it right, for only when there is no sense of self is there perfect clarity. That is true meditation.

I know it sounds extremely abstract and esoteric, but science has already proven that the sense of self is merely a perception that can be transcended. The ego, as we experience it, is a result of areas of the brain known as the default mode network. When we relax sufficiently into meditation, our brainwaves go deeper than alpha — into theta wave or delta wave, for example. At that time, the activity of the default mode network decreases, which results in a transcendence of the sense of self. We may then feel that we are connected to the universe or that we are the universe.

The feeling of connectivity indicates that we are experiencing true meditation and no longer doing meditation.

Of course, as we begin the practice, a large percentage of our time will be spent doing meditation with occasional glimpses of actual meditation, which is represented by feelings of unity. As we persist, the percentage of time that we experience unity will increase as our effort decreases.

The self wants to feel control, and meditation is a kind of release of control, so quite naturally, the mind will resist the meditative process. If we believe the mind's resistant narrations and feelings, we may be deterred from the meditative process. The trick is to relax more and be less concerned about what the mind is telling us. To expedite the process, we might also stop concerning ourselves over other people's opinions about us. Just move forward doing what is healthy and beneficial without concern for opinions, yours or others'.

I sometimes feel tremendous anxiety when I practice the Warrior's Meditation. Why is that?

Your question may relate to the prey-mode of the nervous system, which we discussed to some degree earlier. Allow me to go into more depth on this topic.

There can be several reasons for this anxiety. One reason may be that you believe, consciously or unconsciously, that opening up energetically creates vulnerability — a common New Age teaching. The teaching is true with regard to opening up emotionally, for doing that certainly makes one vulnerable to people who might take advantage of your emotional states. But opening up awareness should not be likened to emotions. Feeling (awareness) should not be equated with feelings (emotions). Opening up feeling actually strengthens us because we come out of our shell, which means we are now facing life fully because, at a nervous system level, we know we are capable of facing life fully. Armoring ourselves is a signal that we are weak and that we do not believe we are capable of handling life fully. The body language created when we close off is an advertisement to predators that you are potential prey.

Instead of blaming predators for taking advantage, it is wise first to take note of the feelings and body language that attracts predators. Once we are aware of what draws these individuals, we can then make conscious corrections to end our own habits. With this conscious approach to inner correction, we will find that our very presence wards off predators, because the way we stand, move, talk, and so forth appears full and capable. The last thing a predator wants is to attack a capable individual, for a predator wants an easy target.

Think of all the people in the world whom you most admire. Those individuals are almost certainly not shelling off. They are probably living authentic lives — the kind of life that you wish you could live. Live authentically, and you will be the person you were born to be.

The second reason that we might feel anxiety when we meditate is because, when we meditate, our bodies go into a kind of healing mode, which naturally brings up unconscious, stuck emotions and mental patterns to be seen and consciously experienced.

Whenever we experience something in life that we emotionally flinch from, it creates a disharmonious psychological imprint that is telling our nervous system we are not good enough to face reality. This unconscious narrative will re-present in our daily lives and in our dreams as feelings of insecurity or anxiety and thoughts of our insufficiency. Surprisingly, these inner imprints can also create narcissistic feelings of our superiority, which is just a way of hiding from the insecurity. Think of people who always have to win to feel good about themselves. What they are not seeing is that they do not feel good about themselves. The competitiveness may just be a cover for unconscious stuckness.

The solution is not to feed the inner critic or the narcissist, but instead to disbelieve any opinions of you — regardless of the source — and return your attention to awareness. The process of restructuring the brain and releasing imprints will take time. It's not a race. Just keep at it unflinchingly, and eventually the brain will stop fighting the process. The brain is seeking to conserve energy, so as soon as it knows you won't give up, it will. It's like a bar fight. If you can keep any attackers engaged for a minute or two without getting hurt, they will be so exhausted that they will be begging you not to hurt them. Likewise the mind will submit to awareness if we are persistent.

The problem is that our mind tends to project the idea that whatever we are feeling now will last forever. If life is pleasant for a long enough period, your mind will acclimate and expect it to last forever; when things become unpleasant, the mind rebels. Similarly, when things are extremely unpleasant, the mind tends to project that the condition will last forever, which creates even more suffering. The truth is that all things pass. Remaining persistent with your meditation practice is the key to inner clarity. The mind will eventually surrender.

Who are you to teach meditation? I think only those who have been given permission to teach meditation from a qualified meditation teacher through a tried and true tradition should be allowed to teach meditation.

I am no one special. Either you experience what I am saying, or you do not. It's completely up to you. In the final analysis, you are responsible for the quality of your life. That said, many times new inventions come from outsiders. Consider that the revolutionary theory of physics, the General Theory of Relativity, was created by Albert Einstein, who was a patent clerk at the time. His theory was roundly rejected at its outset because he was not considered to be an authority on the topic. He had not received the stamp of approval from big names in the field. Time eventually proved him right.

You might find something in the TEM approach that is helpful to you. You can never know if you do not explore this approach thoroughly.

Chapter 14

Meditation Mindset

Many attitudes are inherent to the beta brainwave state. When these attitudes emerge, they tend to keep us in a beta wave state or pull us back to it. In this chapter, we discuss the most common attitudes that create struggle during our meditation sessions. With awareness of these unhelpful attitudes and a little practice at noticing them when they arise within us during meditation and in daily life, we can begin to transcend them.

When unhelpful attitudes arise, our first instinct may be to judge ourselves or get frustrated, but neither is a helpful response. The thing to keep in mind about attitudes is that they stem from existing neural pathways, which means that fighting them or wishing them away is not effective because they are coming from our biology. Our brains are simply doing what they know how to do best, and in many cases, the attitudes that our brains have learned best run counter to awareness and health.

Transcendence of unhealthy attitudes occurs only as a result of an actual change in the brain through neuroplasticity. Because we are aiming to be calmly, yet vibrantly aware in our meditations, returning to calm awareness, no matter what occurs within us, is key, for only by reaching that state will unhealthy neural pathways not be reinforced while we sleep. Instead, the brain will begin to remove resources from the unhealthy neural pathways and allocate those resources to the mapping that enable calm awareness.

The takeaway: no matter what happens, just aim to return to calm awareness. If you find that you are unable to return to calm awareness immediately, that is all right. Just aim to return to calm awareness as soon as you can. Practicing calm awareness in this way will, over time, makes that option increasingly available to you. Eventually, calm awareness will be the most empowered option you have, and thus, it will be your default way of being. This way of being is well worth the time it takes to achieve, no matter how long it takes. Just keep at it persistently; it will happen.

Perfectionism

Although we touched on this topic earlier, I feel there is still more to discuss regarding perfectionism. "Am I doing this correctly?" is one of the most common questions I get after teaching someone to meditate. After we start anything new, it is totally natural to feel awkward and doubt our performance.

To alleviate doubt, I often say, "You feel that way because you certainly are not doing it correctly. It is impossible for you to meditate correctly, for you cannot do meditation. Once you have had enough truly meditative experiences, you will begin to realize that during meditation, there is no you doing it, for awareness has transcended your sense of self."

What I have just stated may seem empty or circular, but really it is nothing of the sort, for surely you have already had moments in your life when there was no sense of self.

Some obvious experiences wherein the self can slip away are while receiving bodywork. If sufficient relaxation occurs during a bodywork session, for example, you may notice that there is a gap of time during which only sensory feeling occurs — but no thought. It's a fantastic feeling.

Furthermore, the sense of self and thought might disappear when we are doing something so intense that there is no time for mental activity, such as when playing a fast-paced sport or video game, or when rock climbing, skydiving, or bungee-jumping. Any intense activity can overwhelm the mind, leading to gaps in thought and the absence of self. Another common way in which thought and self quiet is when we are deeply appreciative of something. Take, for example, a truly captivating fragrance. When a fragrance fills your being, you are lost in the experience.

Many ways are open to us if we wish to lose the sense of self and thereby feel life more directly. Deep relaxation, appreciation, and intense engagement in activity are but a few ways in which we have already experienced a loss of self. If we ask ourselves why we enjoy whatever it is that we enjoy, we may discover that the loss of self during the particular activity is what we are truly enjoying.

When the self slips away, we find that life is much more vibrant and spacious. We find a kind of freedom that is revealed only when the sense of self is not there. The freedom that we feel is the temporary release from our habitual mindset and accumulated mental/emotional baggage.

True meditation is the embodiment of vibrant, spacious freedom — the absence of self. So I repeat, "You cannot do meditation." You will certainly try for a time, and that is as it should be. Just keep doing meditation, and, little by little, larger and larger gaps of no self can emerge, when you are not doing anything, yet awareness is happening. As those no-self experiences repeatedly occur in your life through the process of intentional meditation, periods of spaciousness — "no-mind" — will emerge spontaneously more often during your daily life.

Accept that you will continue to feel doubt about your meditative process for a time. Simply continue to meditate regardless of awkwardness or doubt. Over time, such concerns will fade quite naturally.

With a relaxed, persistent attitude, the sense of self will soften ever more, and your meditations will begin to feel more natural. One day you will realize that even when you experience doubt, it no longer has a dominating effect over your decisions and actions in the world, which is an incredibly liberating state that will fuel you toward an ever more vibrant, fulfilling life.

Expectation

On occasion, when meditating for the first time, an individual has a tremendous, mind-blowing experience that at least, for a while, changes their entire perspective on reality. Invariably, the individual emerges from the experience absolutely on fire about the value of meditation; that is, until their next meditation session, which pales in comparison. Usually such individuals try again and again for a few weeks or months in hopes of re-experiencing the power of that amazing meditation, but it eludes them. Often, within a few months of that first experience, the individual gives up in frustration. The frustration stems from an expectation that cannot be met, because of the nature of meditation.

As an instructor of meditation, I maintain the hope that an initiate has a tangibly meaningful meditative experience, but I caution individuals who have transcendent experiences early in their practice. Imagine how you would feel if, during your first meditation, you experienced absolute, blissful oneness with the universe for a time before returning to your normal sense of self. Under such circumstances, it is only natural to wish for and even ache to return to that blissful state. It is totally understandable that you would feel tremendous frustration when you try again and again in hopes of returning to that condition, only to fail miserably each time.

Under the influence of such powerful desire and expectation, it is easy to understand why you might want to give up. And that is often what happens.

Generally speaking, individuals who have less intense experiences are more likely to continue with the practice than are individuals who hit a home run on day one. In the long run, the person who shows up every day can benefit far more than can the person who had one great experience and quits. Although meditation can be very helpful even in the short term, its greatest dividends are earned over long practice, because the brain needs time to adjust neural pathways to allow for ever greater awareness.

What is it about expectation that blocks us from meditation? If we define meditation as the experience of being fully present, then we can begin to understand why expectation manifests such a powerful blockage. After all, expectation by definition is anticipating a future outcome based upon past experience. So long as we hold on to expectation, there can be no true awareness of the present. Therefore, if we hold strong expectations, even if we follow the steps of the meditative process exactly, we cannot experience being present.

One of the great advantages of the human mind, when compared to the minds of other animals, is its ability to create abstract goals. Our incredible ability to aim for the future is in part what has allowed us to so dominate the resources of the planet. Yet for every advantage, there is an equal and opposite disadvantage. Our relatively strong ability to think is what keeps us from being consciously present, at least until we begin to transcend the power of expectation.

Counterintuitively, transcendence of expectation cannot be realized when we try to stop expectation. The very attempt to forestall this way of thinking requires intensive use of the mind, which will result in a strong beta wave state. A brain in beta wave is not capable of experiencing the present.

Although many ways exist to bypass the mind and experience the present, most of those means are energy intensive and lead to exhaustion, which makes them impractical options in daily life. To conserve energy, relaxing the mind into awareness is the most efficient means of being present. Relaxing into present awareness requires an attitude of acceptance, even toward things that can prove unpleasant ... expectation, for example.

Fighting with expectation will only cause more mental noise, more struggle, and conversely less present awareness. Instead of fighting expectation, soften it without trying to stop it. Expectation, by its nature, is hard, so softening it just a little shifts its energy and converts it into something else. The shift in energy can be likened to the difference between the prepositions *to* and *toward*. *To* is exclusive, cutting out all other possibilities in its hard aim. *Toward* is inclusive, allowing for exploration as one meanders along the path in the general direction of the goal. Modern humans tend to be addicted to a *to* mindset, but animals are more inclined to employ a *toward* mindset.

The difference between to and toward mindsets is readily visible when we watch a typical person walking a dog off leash. The person goes directly to their distant goal, while a dog tends to meander here and there, sniffing and enjoying the sensations of the moment. To meditate, it helps to have the exploratory spirit of toward.

No matter how amazing or difficult your past experience, and no matter how much you wish for a change, it is wise to practice softening expectation, for it is not an ally to presence.

Normalization

One of the advantages of the human mind is its ability to normalize experience. *Normalization* describes the mind's way of making something seem uninteresting to us after we have a certain amount of experience with it. From a survival perspective, normalization makes sense, as it keeps human beings searching for new territories and resources. If humans continually used the same trails and hunted exactly the same lands, they would eventually strip the land of its vitality and starve.

There is, however, a disadvantage to normalization that can cause havoc in our lives. Normalization fuels the consumer society we live in. Consider how people spend money needlessly to buy a newer version of something that already works fine. They will justify the new purchase by pointing out all the new options that it brings, but in reality, they may not actually need the new thing and instead just want it. The problem is only that the old item has lost luster in the mind, and the mind tends to crave something new and fresh because that makes us feel alive. The tendency is not much different than that of a drug habit. It makes us feel good temporarily, but as a default it has a long-term negative effect in our lives.

If you pay attention to the energy of normalization as you experience it; no matter what you purchase, before too long it will begin to feel old to you.

The same normalization process occurs with frequently consumed food: our enjoyment and appreciation can begin to wane, causing us to seek more extreme or unusual tastes.

Normalization causes us to slowly but surely add more sugar to our sweets, which deadens our sensitivity to sugar, so we need to add still more sugar to taste the sweetness. This tendency explains the rampant levels of obesity and diabetes in many modern societies. Many of these diseases result primarily from a lack of sensory awareness amid the unconscious normalization process.

No matter how amazing an experience is, if you do it enough, the mind will begin to normalize to it — even sex. In fact, pornography becomes ever more extreme in large part because of the desire for a "new" experience that will make us truly feel something. The need for ever greater intensity comes from the mind's tendency to normalize experience and from being out of touch with awareness.

Normalization certainly serves an evolutionary purpose, but it is one of the biggest hurdles to the meditative process, as the mind quickly bores of doing the same thing repeatedly. One definition of the meditative state I quite like is that meditation is a condition that does not normalize. If the experience that you are referring to as meditation normalizes for you, then you are not actually achieving a meditative state.

The way to begin freeing yourself from the unhelpful aspects of normalization is to give up the idea that you have already done something. To this end, we can play a little game that will aid in overcoming the unconscious tendency.

Whenever practicing the Warrior's Meditation — or any meditation, for that matter — imagine you are a fresh spirit that just entered the body. Imagine that you have no memory of having ever been in physicality before.

From the perspective of your pure spirit, you know no fear. You do not know anything about survival, about time, about schedules, or about the self. Although you have access to all the memories of the body that you are in, they do not in the least feel like they are your memories, for you are not identified with those memories. They feel to you as if they are someone else's memories. You know how to move the body and get around based on those memories, but the entire process feels totally new and foreign to you from an experiential stance.

For all intents and purposes, you are totally alien to physicality. Thus, being in the physical realm is a very curious experience in which you take profound interest. From this place of innocent curiosity, explore the senses consciously, going through the steps of the Warrior's Meditation.

- Eyes
- Ears
- Nose
- Mouth
- Body
- Spherical awareness

Don't overthink it, just role-play, as if you knew absolutely nothing about the body or physicality. Play with it and have fun!

Willfulness

Willfulness, often prized in society, runs counter to the TEM meditative process, as willfulness stems from a high beta wave brain state. Of course it stands to reason that a productivity-based society would prize such a trait, but becoming addicted to a bullish mindset can prevent us from tapping into the deeper awareness that gives life its color and vibrancy. If willfulness becomes a default stratagem in our lives, it causes suffering.

The trick with meditation is to follow the ten percent rule, which says, "Use no more than ten percent of your attention to focus on any particular thing during meditation." What the ten percent rule really means is that you try to use as little effort as possible while meditating. Of course, as your brain acclimates to meditation over time, less and less effort is required to meditate. Eventually, meditation will be as natural as breathing.

In general, being forceful is not a very good way to work with any living being. If you speak forcefully with your spouse, it probably won't go very well. If you speak forcefully with co-workers, the same is true. When training animals, too much reliance on force can break their spirits.

Counter to what is often taught, we are not trying to break the spirit of ego during meditation, because that very attitude comes from ego. The attempt to stop the ego by condemning it is akin to a dog chasing its own tail.

In large part the meditative process is about softening willfulness through ever-increasing awareness. Because forcefulness generally runs counter to the meditative process, at some point in our practice, we need to find another motivator, another power to move us along.

The secret to transcending willfulness during meditation is found in right attitude, which is a fundamentally innocent, fully engaged curiosity about the entirety of what is happening within and around us right now.

How do we cultivate this innocent, fully engaged curiosity? When I was living in Japan, my wife took me to visit Mutsugoro-san, the famous Japanese "animal whisperer." Mutsugoro-san had a large piece of land in the mountains of Japan, where he helped animals of all sorts recover from abuse and injury. He had a way of communicating with all creatures, even wild animals, that could shift them from a state of aggression to more cooperative states of mind. To see how well his approach worked proved extremely inspiring.

A documentary on Mr. Mutsugoro shows him visiting a Turkish ranch that was being protected from wolves by Kangal dogs, large animals that belong to a livestock protection breed. One of the dogs there was extremely aggressive toward strangers and dangerous, so the family kept him chained in a barn while outsiders visited.

Mr. Mutsugoro wanted to visit this dog, but the family was fearful that it would attack this stranger. He assured the family that he would be fine, and with their permission, he went to see the dog with his camera crew.

As soon as Mr. Mutsugoro came within sight of the dog, it charged him aggressively, barking, snarling, and baring teeth. A thick chain was the only thing keeping that powerful animal from tearing into Mr. Mutsugoro.

Just beyond its biting range, Mutsugoro-san took a playful stance and started moving his hands quickly around the dog's head in a lighthearted fashion. The dog took a few aggressive bites, missing Mr. Mutsugoro's hands before shifting into play mode himself. To everyone's astonishment, within a minute, Mutsugoro-san was petting the dog.

When we think of meditation, we tend to imagine an extremely disciplined, serious activity. But that mindset is sure to result in a lot of mental resistance for many individuals. Shifting our attitude into engaged curiosity — as Mutsugoro-san did — is the secret to a smoother, more enjoyable meditation process for individuals who are resistant to the disciplined approach.

Before beginning meditation, notice the mood of the body and the mindset. If the body feels heavy and the mindset too tight, then it is wise to shift it, much in the way that Mutsugoro-san did with the dog. With a little exploration and practice, you can find more often than not that you, too, are able to shift into a lighter mood.

The way to make this shift is to first pause and take note of how you feel and then decide to soften your feeling. Simply choose to be more curious about where you are, what you are doing, and how you are feeling, and allow your posture to reflect that feeling. Your brain chemistry is highly influenced by how you hold your body, so by changing your posture, you change your emotional state as well.

There will be times when shifting into curiosity through mere intention and posture may seem impossible, so in such instances, just add to the number of vagal breaths that you take during the first stage of the meditative process until the shift naturally occurs. Vagal breathing will shift you out of the high beta wave that is associated with willfulness into a relaxed, yet engaged, conscious alpha wave.

As we explore meditation from a place of engaged curiosity, we gain ever more awareness and trust in the process and our ability to flow with life itself. With continued and engaged practice, inspiration, confidence, clarity, and joy that have little to do with ego, the logical mind, or our accomplishments can emerge.

These new powers will enable us to do what we never before believed possible. We will be more able to accept life as it comes and move harmoniously with it, seeing each moment as an opportunity to engage with life and trust it all the more.

Keep it simple, enjoy it, and keep at it.

Chapter 15

Dealing with Mental Resistance

Even though the Warrior's Meditation is surprisingly easy to practice, we may still find it challenging from time to time. We may feel the temptation to give up on difficult days, but that is the last thing we want to do, for to give up is like telling the brain, "If you throw a tantrum or feel bored, I will stop doing healthy things that make you uncomfortable."

The brain is always seeking comfort. What is comfortable to the brain is usually what it is already acclimated to — old perception habits, limiting beliefs, and normalized emotional baggage. So long as those patterns are maintained, there can be no positive change in our brain pattern and, therefore, no positive change in our lives. Making the brain uncomfortable in useful ways, even if for only short durations, is the key to improving our quality of life.

So, let's imagine you are a beginner and you have decided to sit every morning in open-eyed meditation for fifteen minutes, which is a solid goal. Imagine that around the five-minute mark, you start feeling anxious or bored, and your brain is aching for some relief. Maybe it wants you to eat something, to check social media or email, have a drink or a smoke, to call someone, or to turn on some music — anything that distracts attention from the uncomfortable feelings that the brain is experiencing. Instead of allowing your brain the escape, just sit there for the remainder of the session, aiming to be spatially aware.

If you have to fidget, then fidget, but aim to fidget less and less as you sit there. Just be there without allowing the escape. Face the discomfort and don't worry about how you feel during the meditation period. Instead, notice how you feel after the meditation and during the rest of your day.

What you will discover, with some experience, is that facing the discomfort is actually empowering! And, with that realization, you will start to actively seek out what challenges your ability to meditate, so that you can challenge your brain.

As you start facing discomfort, your definitions of discomfort will begin to soften, such that what used to trigger you and knock you out of awareness grows less challenging. You will be able to handle previous stressors with ease and grace as your brain becomes more open and pliant.

You may begin to notice that you are more able to remain calm and clear in emergency situations that used to cause panic. And that ability will change the way other people see you.

Applying this approach, you will quite naturally start to appear to others as a strong leader. As a result, your social life may start to change for the better, as you embrace new roles, responsibilities, and challenges, and you assist others to do likewise.

Some symptoms of your brain trying to evade the meditation process are incessant thinking, seemingly overwhelming urges and compulsions, brain fog (wherein you seem to forget what you are trying to pay attention to), inner narratives about your self-worth (positive or negative), and feelings of discouragement and doubt.

Bear in mind, the brain tends to think that whatever it is feeling now will last forever, and that illusion creates much of our sense of discomfort. All of these symptoms of avoidance are illusions of a sort that block awareness if you allow them to take over.

If we simply shift our attitude about discomfort, then our psychological reaction provides us with a perfect roadmap for our inner transformation. For example, you might notice that your brain is afraid of small, enclosed spaces. The fear has effectively informed you of your next step to a healthier life, which is to meditate in ever smaller, ever more enclosed spaces until your brain is completely relaxed and open to that experience. But when you succeed once, do not assume that the brain has fully digested the transformation. Challenge the same fear multiple times on different occasions and in different settings, so that your brain can fully transform the fear into awareness.

Facing fears in this way is incredibly empowering. What you are likely to discover through the process of facing and overcoming a fear or phobia is that the triumph has a cascading, positive effect in your life, opening up new potentials and abilities that you never knew you had.

Neural pathways in the brain are connected by association, so with each fear or phobia, countless interconnections run between associated feelings and experiences. These associations can have the unexpected effect of suppressing certain abilities that do not, on the surface, seem to be related to the fear, because those abilities are connected to the fear or phobia via indirect paths in the brain. Once the neural pathways that support the fear or phobia die off, those formerly connected areas are freed up to associate in new ways. We may find that we think more clearly and are more confident.

For example, suddenly, after overcoming a fear of elevators, you might discover that you are no longer afraid to ask out that person whom you have been avoiding for so long, even though you've been thinking about them almost constantly. You just feel inspired to do it, and you do, and as a result your entire life changes. Or you might finally get up the gumption to talk to your boss about that raise you feel you deserve — and you do.

You may find you are able to do things that you previously thought you could not do. What's more, previously unknown talents may suddenly emerge.

New confidence transforms your relationships, releasing you from codependent energies such as territoriality, expectation, false obligation, and desperation. You may find that you are much more present in your relationships, which allows them to flourish and become more engaging than would ever have been possible were you still motivated by clinginess, territoriality, expectation, and false obligation.

Raising children in awareness will enable them to be inspired, emotionally stable, strong, independent, and highly capable individuals — people whom you would love to be around. Likewise, running a business from a place of deep, contextual awareness will provide the greatest possible opportunities for long-term success, as your employees, partners, et cetera feel it a pleasure to work with you.

It all begins by simply remaining aware, even when your brain wants out. Yes, the brain is likely to fill your mental screen with various uncomfortable images and narratives about your past and future, about who you are and how much you're worth or not worth. Know that there is no benefit to believing those thoughts and feelings, and if you simply do not believe those mental projections, you find that there is no need fight against them anymore.

When you notice the mind starts playing those manipulative games, simply return your attention to the meditative process. There is a strong chance that you may believe those images and narrations early on, and that's all right, for that is probably what your brain is used to doing. Just know that both believing and fighting the narrations of the mind feeds the existing pattern.

The images and the narrations are not the truth of you but are, instead, just the established pattern of your brain and the projections which that pattern must express out of habit. Know that those habits are limiting you, but also know that you have power over them simply by not feeding them. For if a neural pathway is not reinforced with your attention, then the brain will take resources away from that pathway and allocate those resources to whatever it is that you are paying attention to. If you are practicing TEM, your attention would be empowering a balanced, broad, contextual awareness.

So when you notice the brain playing out old patterns, simply pause, take note of what is happening and return to spatial awareness. Doing that is the most efficient way to weaken the old pattern and stimulate the brain to construct a more aware, functional pattern.

Our brains may not always afford us pleasant experiences, but living according to what is pleasant or unpleasant, what we like or dislike, is what has largely been limiting us. The solution is to embrace what is healthy and necessary, even if it is uncomfortable or our brains tell us it is unpleasant.

The key to maximizing our capacity to modify our brain through neuroplasticity is found in conscious daily application of our attention toward the changes that we wish to make in our lives. Even just a few minutes a day of dedicated attention to awareness can have a profound impact upon our brains over time.

Once we are aware that the brain changes as a result of how we use our attention, we become masters of our inner transformation, for we are then able to have a greater range of options in response to any particular condition. It matters not if the condition is internal, like the unhealthy narrations that the brain generates based upon its current pattern, or if the condition is external, like an unexpected life result or an incorrigible person. We can make productive changes in our brains that positively alter the way that we perceive stressors and our reactions to stressors.

The secret to inner transformation is actually found in our awareness of our brains' habitual attitude toward what happens within us and without. An attitudinal shift away from "This should not be happening" toward "This is exactly what is happening, and my attitude toward it is my transformational opportunity" is the key to inner transformation.

What you are likely to discover is that every circumstance arrives accompanied by an inner narrative, a brain pattern that may be causing undue suffering for you or for others. It doesn't matter whether it is an unexpected relationship breakup, a business loss, or the death of someone whom you love dearly, for the form of the suffering is less important than the attitude we take toward it.

For example, the brain may lament, "Why did she leave me? I thought she was my soulmate." What the brain is actually saying would more accurately translated as, "I thought I owned her. She should be mine. I need her to be happy," which is an extremely weak, codependent narrative.

Many of our expectations about relationships are just mental projections that reflect a deep inner insecurity related to our self-worth.

We will discover that we are far better off with the attitude that we are choosing to be with someone each moment that we are with them, and they are choosing to be with us, and that it is okay for either party to choose not to be in that relationship at any time. Not believing the mind's unhealthy projections is the key, and then choosing more healthy attitudes is the path to a healthy mind and freedom in meditation.

Chapter 16

Developing Flexibility

As with any meditation, TEM can become a prison if we practice it in the same way every time, for the brain is always looking to create a habit so that it does not have be aware. That being the case, one of the main purposes of TEM is to stretch your brain and keep it pliant, while also tuning your awareness to your deepest, truest inner being, so that you can remain in touch with that inner being throughout the activities of your daily life. If you become overly patterned by any form of meditation, your brain will not have the flexibility to remain aware during your active daily life.

In this chapter we explore flexible ways to practice the Warrior's Meditation by breaking the pattern. The idea of breaking the pattern fits with the Ha phase of Shuhari, the natural progression of learning. In the Ha phase, we want to shift the training pattern around in as many ways as possible, so that we are constantly being exposed to new possibilities and new applications.

Once we get the hang of the basic order of the Warrior's Meditation and able to get into a conscious alpha state consistently, we are wise to intentionally change the order of the meditation steps; how long we spend between each step; the way that we sit, stand, or move during meditation; et cetera, to keep the brain from developing a rigid neural pattern. The result is a highly aware, flexible, healthy brain.

The first pattern to break has to do with our eyes. If, for example, we practice the Warrior's Meditation daily for months on end with the eyes open, as the most basic practice recommends, we understand without a doubt that we can easily meditate with our eyes open, but we might be shocked to discover that we are unable to meditate with eyes closed thanks to the brain's newly developed association between meditation and having the eyes open.

It might seem counterintuitive that we would have an easier time meditating with our eyes open than we would with our eyes closed, but all else being equal, what is easy for us depends largely on how we practice. The human brain patterns itself in the same ways as does a dog's brain — through association. If, for example, we conduct a dog's training to sit inside the house, we may be surprised to discover that the dog does not obey the sit command when outside. The dog is not necessarily being disobedient, although we may be quick to assume that is the case.

What occurs in such circumstances is that the dog's brain associates the sit command with being in the house. When we go outside, the brain does not have the right context to access the neural pathway of sit when we utter the command, so the dog is confused.

To overcome this challenge, we need to revisit the sit command when the dog is outside the house until the dog's brain makes the new association. We might also find that we need to teach it again when we are off our property, when we are in someone else's house, and so forth. After breaking the in-house sit pattern enough times with alternate variations, the brain becomes flexible with the concept of *sit*, and then the dog can sit on command anywhere.

Just as with the dog's brain, we need to teach our brains to see the overall meaning of meditation, so that they can do it easily anywhere and under any circumstance.

Once you are acclimated to the Warrior's Meditation and able to consistently get into a meditative state with the method, we will want to learn to do the practice with eyes closed. We can use the basic steps of the Warrior's Meditation to accomplish this aim.

Go through the six steps of the Warrior's Meditation, but only give about a minute per step — eyes, ears, nose, mouth, body, spherical awareness. Once you have gone through all the steps and are in a solid meditated state, try closing your eyes and maintaining the expanded feeling. If you feel somehow smaller when you close your eyes, it indicates that you are falling out of the meditation state. In that case, simply open your eyes and reconnect with the expanded feeling. Once you re-establish a meditative awareness, try closing the eyes again. Repeat this process until you feel a seamless transition between the open-eyed and closed-eye meditation.

Do not assume, however, that the brain has fully made the association yet. The next day, when you practice meditation, be sure to try it with your eyes closed to see how the brain reacts. Chances are you will need to repeat the transitional training again a few times to reinforce the new association.

Once you become equally proficient with both eye options, just switch it up each day, sometimes with eyes open at the beginning of the meditation practice and sometimes waiting until later in the meditation steps to open the eyes. As I said, we want to play with the Warrior's Meditation in as many ways and in as many varying situations as possible, so that the brain learns to allow for meditation at any time under any circumstance.

With flexibility in mind, once you are able to meditate consistently while sitting, start practicing meditation from a standing position. Once you are good at standing, change from standing to sitting in the middle of meditation, or vice versa. Try meditating while walking, then while jogging, then while running. Try it while swimming or weightlifting. Try it while performing hobbies. Try it while in conversation, which is one of the hardest challenges for beginners.

If, when challenging yourself in these flexible ways, you notice that you are falling back into a beta wave, nonmeditative state, dial back the challenge a little until you are again solidly in a conscious alpha wave state. Once back in alpha, challenge yourself again. It might take several tries to overcome a challenge, such as rising from a seated position to a standing position while in meditation, but the result is well worth the effort.

Hiccups and failures are a natural and necessary part of development with any skill or ability. I have found over my years of teaching that, with practice and patience, everyone gets it. The most important thing to keep in mind is that the brain must fail before it can refine any ability. Have no concern for how many times it takes to overcome a challenge. Just enjoy the process.

With a positive attitude toward challenges, you will discover that there is nothing that you can't do while in a state of meditation, apart from selfishly lying, cheating, or maintaining negative emotional and mental patterns. To be aware and healthy, we have to sacrifice something.

Chapter 17

Mental Maps and the Stages of Competence

Meditation, unlike almost every other human activity, does not really require the accumulation of knowledge the way other processes of learning do, although there certainly is a familiarity curve when we first begin practicing. Instead, meditation is really about getting in touch with awareness and the transcendence of our resistance to internal and external challenges — acceptance.

The brain is a very energy-intensive organ. For the average person with a 2000 calorie per day diet, the brain would burn about 300 of those calories. To conserve energy, the brain tries to do less. It takes quite a lot of energy to change the brain, so by default the brain resists change to some degree.

Wise individuals are careful not to allow the brain to become too resistant, for the "lazy" tendency of the brain to resist new perspectives may be more harmful than helpful in many circumstances, if left unchecked.

We all have three primary mental maps that provide scaffolding for our perception. These maps give us a familiar sense of our values — who we are and where we fit in society. Surprisingly, if the lazy tendency of the brain goes unchecked, it matters little whether our inner maps are very accurate or not, for the brain is primarily looking to conserve energy. Maintaining the existing maps is comfortable for the brain, whereas changing them is stressful. Left unchecked, the brain will most certainly choose comfort.

Here are the three primary maps of the mind:
1. Self-image — how we see ourselves
2. Social status — what others expect of us
3. Beliefs — what we believe to be true

When we are first conceived and still in the womb, we do not have a brain. At this initial stage of cellular development, a process called cellular metabolism serves to separate nutrients from toxins, so that the cells can grow and replicate safely.

Once the body develops a digestive system, the same principle applies to the gastrointestinal process. Things become wonky once the individual develops a sense of self, for the sense of self can depart from the separation of nutrient from toxin as it assigns value and focus, instead, on the pleasant and the unpleasant, often resulting in a choice for comfort over health. It doesn't matter as much to the brain that the pleasant might be toxic or the unpleasant might be nutritious, for it is fundamentally seeking to maintain a comfortable neurological pattern, so that it doesn't have to pay attention, which is an energy-intensive activity.

At this stage of development the brain is typically less interested in facts or truth than in maintaining its mental maps, which is why most people are generally less interested in facts or truth than they are interested in having their current perspectives and beliefs reinforced.

Again, because the brain is seeking to conserve energy, its primary tendency is to resist anything that does not fit into its current set of mental maps. For this reason, we tend to feel anxiety or frustration when our maps do not jibe with reality.

The tendency to resist should not be condemned, but for individuals who seek to improve the fundamental quality of their life, it is highly beneficial to be aware of our brain's tendency to reject change, for only when we are aware of this default tendency are we be able to challenge the tendency at appropriate times.

If we pay attention, we notice that people often doing things that they know are unhealthy. We also notice that people tend not to do things that they know are healthy, preferring instead whatever is entertaining or comfortable. We all know that exercise is good for us, but we might not exercise. We may know that smoking is unhealthy and can lead to premature death and disease, but many smokers remain undeterred. We may know that meditation is a vital practice for our health and well-being, yet we may fail to continue. The reason is that health might not be our mind's primary value. Maintenance of the current maps is the priority, because we feel safe when we are comfortable. Divergence from the familiar feels very uncomfortable.

We all know stubborn, miserable people who would rather die than to give up their current perception of self. At first glance, we may think those people are stupid, but it isn't necessarily a matter of intelligence, for many geniuses fall into the same brain traps.

The second mental map is for social status. We humans, being social creatures, tend to be highly sensitive to how others view us. We may be trying to live up to other people's expectations of us. Many a midlife crisis has its origins in trying to live our lives according to how our parents think we should live; we married someone who doesn't suit us, or we took on a career that proves unsatisfying. Still others among us are desperately seeking to be liked, which is likely to spur us to create false images of ourselves in hopes of garnering approval. All of these urges result from seeking the pleasant and avoiding the unpleasant.

The third mental map focuses on what we believe to be true. This map consists entirely of beliefs and ideologies that feel familiar to us. These ideologies and beliefs could include politics, religion, spirituality, philosophy, and even scientific theories that have become commonly accepted but that we are not interested in questioning — the antithesis of the scientific method.

Living according to these maps can lead us into depression and anxiety when reality smacks us in the face or when we take an honest look at ourselves. When we look, we may see that our maps are incorrect and have been incorrect for most of our lives. For example, you may feel deeply depressed after a divorce because you feel you wasted 20 years of your life with that person. The attitude itself can easily lead us into a psychological crisis, whereas if we just moved on with our lives, having learned the lessons the marriage offered us, there is no reason the divorce need lead to any further negativity — unless, of course, you don't want to learn from your experiences.

When we look deeply and notice something is amiss with our lives, we are likely to feel very uncomfortable. We may unconsciously begin to associate honest, self-observation with dread, and so we are less inclined to look again. In actuality, the long-sustained lack of observation and the life that we built around our false perceptions cause the pain. What's more, the negative attitude that we have when we finally choose to look may feed shame, guilt, blame, doubt, and any number of other unhelpful mental or emotional projections.

In truth, looking is the first step to correcting our lives, but we must look with discernment, not condemnation. You are not your past. Your life is afresh each day, if you are living in awareness. When we live with an unconscious focus on the past, we feel as if awareness is to be feared. If we fear awareness, then our inner development is arrested, for we will be unable to assess our lives honestly.

Now that we are familiar with the three mental maps, we can begin to make healthy changes to those maps with our newfound awareness.

With healthy development in mind, here are the four stages of competence that we go through when our inner maps are in the process of change. Being aware of the four stages of competence can keep us from abandoning the learning process when things become uncomfortable.

Modern psychology describes the four stages of competence as follows:
1. Unconscious incompetence — wrong intuition

2. Conscious incompetence — wrong analysis
3. Conscious competence — right analysis
4. Unconscious competence — right intuition

Unconscious incompetence

At this stage we might not recognize a deficit in competence or understand how to correct the deficit. In fact we may even feel inclined to deny our incompetence or the importance of the knowledge that could correct the incompetence.

To progress to the next stage of learning, which is conscious incompetence, the individual must recognize their dysfunction and the value of the new knowledge. The time it takes to navigate this stage depends on awareness and the level of resistance the individual feels toward the knowledge once they become aware that there is such knowledge.

Unconscious incompetence could be likened either to the childlike state of innocence or a stage of willful ignorance, depending upon whether we have no knowledge or we have false knowledge that brings us comfort.

To get an idea of false knowledge that brings us comfort, think of how children feel about the story of Santa Claus. Children tend to love the idea that Santa comes every Christmas Eve to bring them gifts. Now consider what children feel when they are informed that Santa doesn't exist. When children find out that Santa is not real, they are prone to feel shocked, embarrassed, and depressed. They go through a period of denial until they are teased out of the false perception. The experience of being deceived by their parents and then being teased for their foolishness may cause some to lose trust in the people who instilled the false belief.

If it was socially acceptable, many children would probably continue to believe in Santa even after they were told he was not real, because the story of Santa made them feel so good. In large part, it is the pressure and judgment of society that stimulates a child to abandon belief in Santa.

Before our incompetence is exposed, we are usually unaware of that incompetence and our lack of knowledge. We just don't know what we don't know — it's natural. Although our lack of competence limits our functionality in the world, we do not yet know of our limitation or the possibilities that might open to us by acquiring new knowledge.

At some point we are exposed to new information that demonstrates our lack of knowledge or ability. The exposure challenges our brain's existing pattern by demonstrating that our current perspective is limited in some way.

Conscious Incompetence

Once the individual recognizes their incompetence and the value of the new knowledge, they are at the stage of conscious incompetence (Shu), where the individual does not understand or know how to do something, but they are aiming to correct the deficit.

Making mistakes in the attempt to acquire the new skill or knowledge is required at this stage. The stage of conscious incompetence is an uncomfortable stage for the brain, and it can last for quite some time, depending upon how difficult the new ability or knowledge is to acquire. At this stage, there is still danger that the brain will reject the new knowledge if it seems to be too challenging.

Every time we abandon an old belief or self-image and seek to acquire a new skill, knowledge, or perspective, our brains are rewriting our mental maps. In the long run, it is much healthier to challenge the brain by rewriting the mental maps according to the best possible information, because when we fail to rewrite those inner maps according to reality, we are telling our nervous system and brain that we are not strong enough to face the truth, which is psychologically debilitating.

When reality doesn't align with our maps, and we choose to maintain our maps, we necessarily must turn away from awareness. The result of turning away from awareness is long-term anxiety and imbalance at a nervous system level. Fear takes over our lives and leads us astray, something that can easily lead to an identity crisis later in life.

Although it can be uncomfortable at first, the solution is to soften our beliefs and open ourselves to new perspectives. We are likely to feel extremely awkward when we are at the level of conscious incompetence, as if trying to brush our teeth with our non-dominant hand. But that awkwardness is a sign that the brain is struggling to become flexible and aware. Over the long term, challenging the brain in this way allows the nervous system to relax, because it is now hearing the message, "I am strong enough to move through discomfort and fear."

Conscious Competence

Once we decide to embrace new knowledge and set aside our old perspective, we can begin learning honestly, which leads us to the third stage of learning, conscious competence (Ha).

At this stage we understand how to do something, but proper execution requires concentration. For example, if we were learning to dance, at this stage we could dance, but we have to be attentive to dancing to be sure that our feet are behaving, that we are in rhythm, that we are following the form properly, et cetera. Our abilities at this stage are really quite delicate, for even relatively small distractions can throw us off.

Unconscious Competence

At some point in our practice, the effort will disappear, and dancing will feel totally natural. This naturalness reflects the final stage, which is unconscious competence (Ri). At this stage we can execute our abilities even under severe pressure, because we don't have to think about how to execute — it is "second nature."

The Principle of Acceptance

The ability to soften our mental maps so that we are open to beneficial change is vital to the meditative process. Fundamentally, we are talking about an attitude of acceptance. I would argue that there can be no meditation without acceptance, for fundamentally meditation is the direct experience of nonresistance, which results in relaxed clarity. Thus, meditation is not possible so long as we are fighting to protect old perceptions.

Much of what we have already explored has revealed the limitations of the reader's current mental maps. The danger is primarily for those readers who are well versed in other forms of meditation, who might wonder, "Who is this guy to contradict my teacher, my tradition?"

Don't trust me. I am not an authority. Don't rely on your teacher or your tradition. To trust blindly is to usurp your responsibility to explore life fully and see for yourself. And if you are closed to new perspectives then you also lack acceptance, which will greatly limit your meditations.

When learning something new, it is helpful to set aside all previous notions, at least temporarily, so that you can experience the new approach honestly. If we have a negative feeling toward any information that challenges our current inner maps, we cannot have an honest experience, which means we have prejudged the new before we have truly experienced it.

Even if we temporarily set aside our old paradigm to experience the new, and even if the new proves valuable through our experience, we may feel resistance that resonates with an inner narrative as something like, "You are unraveling my world." The belief is that your world equates with your mental maps. The maps are not your world. They are just an inner tool meant to help you navigate reality. Your true world cannot be contained by any mental map, for the truth of you, like the truth of life, far exceeds your ability to define or map. Do not let the tool become your master.

Meditation is meant to put you in touch with the fundamental you, so that you can directly experience it without interference from the maps of the self. Through direct experience of the fundamental you, there is clarity.

The fundamental you is the pure perception that exists prior to the maps of self, which your brain has unconsciously created throughout your life. No matter how often you experience the fundamental you, the mind will never be able to properly define it, but it will most certainly try, for the mind's pattern is to define and map out all experience.

The fundamental you exists prior to or at a deeper level of the brain than mapping and defining, so it will never fit any specific description. When we can rest in awareness of our fundamental nature without trying to define or map it, then and only then can it be said that we are truly meditating.

The experience of your fundamental nature is truly transformative, for it is the healing element that brings about all the benefits of meditation that we discussed in the Introduction. The fundamental you is the corrective element, the spark of life, the essence of awareness. Embrace it by softening the maps of self, former teachings, and authorities. Intend to experience directly your fundamental nature without preconceived notions, expectation of outcomes, or bias of attention. With interest and direct perception, your fundamental nature can reveal itself.

I'm not suggesting that our mental maps are bad or that we should throw them out. In fact our mental maps provide us with functionality in the world, but they can also very easily become a prison of sorts. The trick is to soften them so that they do not block awareness. Being open to the reality of the moment offers a healthier, more vibrant life, for your brain and nervous system to become highly flexible and receptive to new information and broader perspectives, and that makes you a very clear individual.

Part IV

Daily Life Application

As you can probably see by now, TEM is specifically designed to be incorporated into our daily lives, for as we bring awareness into our daily lives, they are transformed. That stated, transformation is always a two-way street: not only does awareness change daily life for the better, but positive alteration in our daily life pattern also empowers greater awareness. Bearing in mind the reciprocal influence of awareness and our daily life patterns, we can begin to make adjustments on both fronts that lead to a virtuous cycle of positive improvements to our lives.

In Part IV we learn how certain supportive lifestyle changes can help to improve the quality of our meditative experience, as well as the health of our brain and body. We also explore the nature of various emotional biases, which have been unconsciously painting our reality in unhelpful ways. Through noticing those biases as they express themselves, we can begin to free ourselves, which, in turn, improves our lives and our overall awareness.

Once we gain an understanding of our emotional biases, we learn the relationship between posture, breathing, and our emotional states. Through that exploration, you learn to consciously guide your emotional states to expedite your neurological transformation and improve your daily life experience.

After learning how to guide emotions, we discover the secret to the instant meditation ability that the elite Samurai so highly valued. You will find the ability to meditate instantly to be a vital tool in your active daily life, for it will help you to navigate the many stressors you are likely to encounter each day.

From there we highlight the essence of training that is found in the basics, for all higher level expressions of any training are rooted in a solid foundation.

Finally, we explore the guiding philosophy of the Total Embodiment Method (TEM). Through doing so, you learn that TEM is not necessarily a new method, as it might seem, but probably is instead the original, lost meditation of human beings that always reemerges when the human develops in the right physical circumstances.

Chapter 18

Supportive Lifestyle Adjustments

Even with the incredible flexibility and ease of the Total Embodiment Method, numerous lifestyle-related issues can create undue difficulty during meditation. If you maintain these unhelpful patterns, no matter how dedicated you are to your meditation practice, you will see suboptimal results. This chapter is dedicated to pointing out the most common lifestyle-related blockages and helping you find solutions.

Sleep Time and Duration

Quality sleep is absolutely essential to living a vibrant, healthy life, but in the modern world, with all its comforts, we face many persistent causes of suboptimal sleep. If we lack sufficient sleep, meditation sessions can become a struggle just to remain awake for their duration, let alone to be aware.

With the aim of being more aware, it is vital that we maintain a proper sleep biorhythm, a common area of imbalance in modern society. The biorhythm is the schedule of bodily processes. If the time that we lie down to sleep each night varies by more than 30 minutes, it causes sleep quality disturbance. By not keeping a solid sleep schedule, we might have trouble drifting off to sleep and/or achieving sufficient deep sleep cycles to allow the body proper rejuvenation. In such a case, we are likely to be less aware throughout the day, as parts of the brain are not functioning optimally.

A messed-up sleep rhythm can, over time, cause the nervous system to become either over-reactive or under-reactive, potentially resulting in a lot of physical tension and inflammation, as well as loss of memory, inability to focus, and emotional reactivity. When we don't sleep well, the quality and enjoyment of anything we do is compromised.

When you get your sleep cycle right, your sleep quality is likely to improve, and that will improve your emotional state throughout the day, allowing you more graciousness in the face of challenges. With better sleep, you think more quickly and efficiently, have more energy, and are more inspired than you would otherwise be.

Common medical advice says that humans should get an average of eight hours of sleep per night. While that may be true for many people, it does not apply to everyone. Each person has an optimal amount of sleep that can change as we age. When we get significantly more or less sleep than is optimal for us personally, it negatively affects our daily life.

Everyone is different, so the key to discovering your own optimal sleep duration is to pay attention to what generally feels best to you. People with very high energy, for example, may do best with only four of five hours of sleep per night. For such individuals, sleeping longer than four or five hours is unhealthy. Conversely, they may suffer if they get only three hours of sleep. Although many of us can function well if we have one or two nights of five hours' sleep, few of us can sustain that schedule and remain healthy.

Still other people, who may have less energetic bodies, may need more than eight hours' sleep to be healthy. They may function best with nine or ten hours of sleep. The key is to find out what works best for you and stick with it each night, including on weekends.

Do not sleep in or take daily naps to make up for a lack of sleep. Although the occasional nap is good, in general correcting your sleep schedule and keeping it consistent is the best way for the body to recover. Sleeping in tends to throw off the biorhythm and diminish sleep quality overall.

Not sleeping in or taking naps can be a real challenge for individuals who are already deeply sleep-deprived. Keep in mind that sleeping during the day will prevent your body's biorhythm from correcting. The challenge is to stay up until your proper sleep time, and then go to bed. No matter how poorly you sleep that night, get out of bed at a predetermined time and stay up. The biorhythm will correct itself in short order if your sleep schedule is consistently maintained.

I have heard a number of spiritual teachers claim that people should never sleep more than five hours per night, and that an awakened individual does not need sleep at all. The problem with these statements is that, even if true, the claim would apply only to fully awakened individuals and not to the unawakened masses who might be tempted to follow that sleep advice. If our bodies are not naturally tuned to getting just five hours of sleep, our health will be compromised.

Keeping the sleep cycle in tune with the solar cycle is almost as important to getting quality sleep as the amount of time that we sleep. The basic idea is to be sure you awaken an hour or two before sunrise, for that is what you would certainly be doing if you were living a hunter-gatherer life-style.

If the sun rises at 6 AM where you live, aim to awaken at least by 5 AM each day. If you are an eight hour sleeper then that would get you to sleep by 9 PM each night. I know it sounds strange to go to sleep that early, but if you go camping for a week without using any artificial light, you will notice that you get sleepy a lot earlier than you do when you are living at home and being exposed to artificial light constantly. When I camped for a month in a forest without any artificial lights or electronics, I noticed that I got sleepy just about two hours after sundown and awoke naturally about an hour before sunrise every day, like clockwork. I awoke refreshed and ready to start my day. As soon as I returned to Tokyo, my sleeping rhythm changed back to my old pattern, which was to stay up late and get poor quality sleep.

Be careful not to turn sleep into an ideology. Just pay attention to how much sleep your body requires to feel energetic and aware during your day.

Even if you are technically in bed for the number of hours that your body requires to be rested, if you have insufficient sleep quality, you'll still suffer throughout the day. If you are getting sufficient bed time and keeping a solid sleep schedule but you are still not sleeping well, then there are probably other areas, related to the modern lifestyle, that you can correct to help you to sleep better.

Lighting Issues

Lack of sufficient exposure to sunlight during the day can cause your body not to produce enough melatonin, a hormone that brings on sleep. If you are spending too much time indoors, you would be wise to spend a little more time outside, especially in the early morning as the sun is rising, for the sun rising stimulates your body to wake up. If you are not able to get sufficient sun exposure during the day, you might try using a daylight therapy lamp in your work space to stimulate melatonin production.

Several hours before going to bed, be sure to avoid blue and green light, both of which stimulate the brain into wakefulness. Blue light, for example, is generated by most computer and smartphone screens. You can use software on those devices that will shift the light to red after sunset. Red light will not stimulate the brain into a wakeful state the way blue and green light does. Night Shift, Redshift, and Red Moon are great free software choices, depending upon the device you use.

Another related issue may be too much light in your sleeping space. The skin is extremely sensitive to light, so that even a little light touching the skin can stimulate the brain to fall out of sleep. A great way to counter this issue is to purchase blackout curtains for your bedroom and turn off the night light when you go to sleep. You want to sleep in a pitch dark room if at all possible.

Food-Related Sleep Disturbance

If you notice that you have a tendency to awaken in the middle of the night and then have trouble getting back to sleep, some adjustments may help to correct the issue.

The first consideration in nightly wakefulness is when you last consumed any caloric or chemical substance, for those things may cause restlessness. We are wise not to eat or drink any caloric substance three to four hours before going to sleep. To get the highest quality sleep possible, the stomach should be entirely empty of content, so that its weight does not press on other visceral organs and disturb them, which negatively affects sleep.

Many people eat shortly before going to bed because they feel hungry. The problem is probably that they are not consuming enough high-quality fat during the day. Chances are, they're eating too many sugars and processed carbohydrates that digest rapidly and result in a quick return of hunger. Eating more high-quality fats allows for greater satiation and longer energy burns, so that you do not feel hungry before or during sleep.

Scientific studies in the 1940s showed a correlation between high-fat diets and high-cholesterol. The assumptions at the time were that high cholesterol led to heart disease, and high-fat diets were the cause of high-cholesterol. These assumptions led physicians and patients to embrace the low-fat diet for weight loss and heart health.

By the 1960s, the low-fat diet was no longer considered good for just high-risk heart patients, but for everyone. By 1980 the low-fat diet, which was being heavily promoted by physicians, the federal government, the food industry, and the popular health media, became the primary diet of the nation. There was a documented correlation between low-fat diets and weight loss or the prevention of heart-disease, so Americans continued with the low-fat trend. Ironically, while on the low-fat diet, Americans began experiencing an obesity epidemic.

Americans were following the guidelines of the food pyramid, which placed the greatest caloric emphasis on eating high quantities of carbohydrates and little fat. Recently science has acknowledged the error and is beginning to advise a more moderate approach to fats.

The move away from fats resulted in greater consumption of processed carbohydrates and sugars. This caloric shift resulted in steep increases in obesity, heart disease, diabetes, and psychological disorders such as anxiety and depression.

The key to remember with fats is that your brain and your hormones are sourced from fats. If you are not eating a sufficient amount of high-quality fat, then your hormones will be out of balance. High-quality fats include animal fats, nuts, and avocados, for example. Regarding the science on fat, it's still unclear what causes heart disease and what does not. Essentially, there was never any causal connection shown between the consumption of saturated fats and heart-disease. Considering that almost all fat intakes of hunter-gatherers is from animal fat (saturated fats), it makes sense that our bodies would be well adapted to those foods. It's a good idea to discuss fat consumption with your health practitioner, if you feel inclined to change your diet.

Of course consumption of alcoholic drinks, certain medications, and caffeine in the evening can disrupt the sleep cycle, as well. The general rule is to have only water after your last meal of the day.

Night Cramps

If you find that you sometimes wake up at night from cramps, you may not be taking in enough salt with your meals, or you are getting dehydrated while you sleep. To test which is the issue, try a week of keeping water at bedside. You may notice that you tend to wake up just before a cramp starts, so at that time, drink a few ounces of water. If that keeps the cramps from initiating, then you know you are suffering from dehydration. Better daily hydration is your answer.

The basic rule is to have constant access to water that you will sip whenever you feel thirst. Be sure to consume no more than seven ounces (about seven normal swallows) of water in a 15-minute period, for that will stimulate a kidney flush, which is the sudden urge to pee after you have had too much to drink. When drinking stimulates a kidney flush, our bodies are not absorbing the water, so we can still be dehydrated.

If sipping water does not resolve the cramping, then you might try making a half-cup of saltwater to drink after dinner. Salt is an electrolyte. Make the water salty enough that you clearly taste the salt, but not so salty that you are repulsed by it.

Note: increasing salt intake can lead to high blood pressure, which can result in a stroke. If you have high blood pressure, there is a fair chance that you already have too much salt in your diet. In that case, your diet may be lacking in some other electrolyte. You would be wise to consult your health professional to address the issue.

Hot Flashes

Your sleep can also suffer if you are going through menopause, which can cause hot flashes. According to medical science, hot flashes start when blood vessels near the skin's surface widen to cool off. As the vessels widen, we begin to sweat profusely. Some individuals also experience chills and a rapid heart rate.

Many people who are going through menopause experience nighttime hot flashes that jar them out of sleep. Once we are hot and sweaty, it can seem to be nearly impossible to fall back to sleep.

Women most commonly suffer from hot flashes, but men can too. Most men are unaware that they can suffer from hot flashes. And many middle aged men may be waking up from them, but not recognizing that they are having hot flashes. If you are waking up in a sweat multiple times a week, chances are high that you are experiencing hot flashes.

Some relatively effective ways allow us to deal with hot flashes. The first and most obvious is to cool your body down just before going to sleep. You might get into a cool bath, for example. It is also wise to keep the room that you sleep in on the cool side and not use too many covers. You want your body temperature to be just a little on the cool side when you sleep to minimize hot flashes.

Although you may not be able to stop hot flashes entirely, you can do some things to minimize them. Here are some hot flash stimulators: stress, caffeine, alcohol, spicy foods, tight clothing, heat, and cigarette smoke. Reducing these stimulators can go a long way toward curtailing hot flashes.

Once you get a hot flash, you are going to want to get back to sleep as soon as possible. To aid in that purpose, be sure to cool the body by removing some of your covers. You may also find that deep breathing can be very helpful to relax the body so that it can fall asleep again as soon as possible.

Once hot flashes begin, the average person is prone to experience them for seven years, so given time, they are likely to stop occurring even if you do nothing to prevent them.

Wake-Up Plan

How we wake up is just as important as how long we sleep. When we have truly slept well, we tend to pop out of bed with a clear, vibrant mind, ready to start our day. If we have not been sleeping well for an extended period of time, we won't have that pop in the morning. Similarly, if we lack an inspiring reason to get up vigorously each day, we will tend to just lie there for long periods of time, not wanting to get up. Finding a powerful reason to get up each day will help you to get out of bed sooner, which will sharpen the quality of your day as well as the quality of your sleep.

A good way to help get some energy into your morning is to clarify the night before what you are going to do the next morning when you first wake up. You want to set your intention for those activities just before going to bed.

Take a minute to plan your morning. Consider the following elements:
- Wake-up time
- Get up time (try to make it the same as wake up time)
- Urinating
- Stretching
- Coldwater face washing or shower
- Meditation and/or vagal breathing

Of course, you will want to have an inspiring reason to go about your day each day, but that may not be readily available to you from your social environment. After all, many of us work primarily to pay the bills, and we are not doing what inspires us. Although that may be the case for many of us, we still need to have a plan for the time when we arise each morning.

Every night before you go to sleep, set your plan and your intention to pop out of bed and do what is healthy. You will discover if you make your next morning plans the night before and set a powerful intention, that you will get out of bed sooner and with more inspiration to tackle the challenges of the day, and that attitude will enable you to be more engaged each day, which will then lead you to sleep better at night.

Exercise

Getting daily exercise has been shown to help the body to regulate hormones. If you are not exercising sufficiently each day, now is a good time to start. In the absence of sufficient daily exercise, your body will not sleep as well as it would if you were exercising. The impact of exercise on sleep is most noticeable with highly energetic individuals.

Such individuals, if they do not exercise, will tend to be easily agitated or excitable. This excitability will affect not only their relationships but also their sleep quality, for their bodies will simply be unable to relax.

People who are very low on energy also need to exercise to sleep better, for exercise will increase blood flow to the brain and vital organs, which in turn increases health and vitality. Such individuals will sleep better and tend to wake up with more motivation to get out of bed and start the day.

The human body, from an evolutionary perspective, is still a hunter-gatherer body, which means that, to be healthy, it needs to move each day as if it were hunting and gathering. Hunter-gatherers typically walk about five miles per day, and so should we.

Walking is one of the very best activities for the body, for all other bodily systems are toned by the movements of walking. If we are not getting enough exercise, we will not sleep as well, nor will our bodies digest as efficiently as they would if they were well exercised.

Of course, many other exercises can benefit health. Examples include yoga, tai chi, dancing, hiking, swimming, weightlifting, and cardiovascular exercises. If at all possible, try to find an exercise that you enjoy, because that will motivate you to do it every day.

Basically, we want to keep the body flowing through healthy movement. To improve the health of our bodies and brains, we want to be strong and stable, yet flexible, able to handle extremes of weather and humidity.

At some point, your body may become frail from injury or disease. At that time, do what you can to keep it as strong and flexible as possible. If you need to rest, then be sure to rest. There is no need to become overly willful or ideological about exercise. Instead, move toward better health incrementally. As your health gradually improves, you are likely to notice that your sleep quality improves as well.

Healthy Dietary Adjustments

Although we discussed diet earlier, we still have much more to explore in this area. Medical science and psychology are beginning to discover that much of our depression and anxiety comes from our diet.

One of the biggest challenges for a meditator has to do with energy levels. When we eat a lot of carbohydrates and sugars, our blood sugar levels tend to spike, which triggers insulin release, and that causes a blood sugar crash. When our blood sugar crashes, we experience increased agitation, plus reduced mental clarity and awareness.

The idea may seem hard to grasp, but the diet recommended by the American medical community may not be serving you. If you lived as a hunter-gatherer, most of your dietary intake would be in the form of fat and protein. Second to fat and protein would be vegetables. Last in availability would be complex carbohydrates and sugars, because grains and berries are highly seasonal. In short, the hunter-gatherer diet is nearly the polar opposite of the food pyramid's recommendations.

The brain is primarily made up of lipids, which are fats, and so it is vital that we take in quality fats as building blocks for brain cells. Your first meal each day should be fat-and-protein-intensive, which will provide a long, even caloric burn that will keep your energy levels stable throughout the day.

These days, intermittent fasting has become popular. Intermittent fasting is a form that one does every day or every other day. The key to intermittent fasting is that the window of time between the first meal and the last must be no more than 12 hours, to allow your body at least 12 hours without any caloric or chemical intake; this allows the body to burn off stored fat in the liver for energy. If you eat a high-fat diet three meals a day without intermittent fasting, your body will continue to store up cholesterol in the liver and bloodstream, and that may cause your cholesterol levels to skyrocket.

I personally quite enjoy intermittent fasting, because it tracks very closely with how our natural eating cycle would be as hunter-gatherers. Prime hunting times are several hours before and after sunrise and sunset, for those hours are when animals on the day shift return to their dens or lays for sleep and animals on the night shift come out to find food and resources. Nature is at its most active during these solar transition periods, which means as hunter-gatherers, we would be hunting during these times, not eating.

Coming back from your morning hunt, you probably wouldn't eat until 9 or 10 AM. If you ate a fatty, protein-rich meal, you would not be hungry again until seven or eight hours later, when you would eat again before heading out for your evening hunt. You would likely consume nothing other than water outside of those meals.

If you follow the eating schedule that hunter-gatherers do, you are likely to have 16 hours between meals, which is an ideal fasting time. Following this protocol, you might be surprised to find that you are less hungry between meals, you eat less overall, and you enjoy your food much more during mealtime. In the long run, you are likely to have more energy and sleep better when fasting intermittently.

As for vegetables, I personally enjoy them during my evening meal. I try to get as many variations as possible. You might try that strategy to see how it works for you. Here are some great vegetable options based upon color. Getting as many color variations as possible in your diet will provide a wider range of nutrient and phytochemicals to support your health.

Yellow (squashes, bell peppers, grapefruit, bananas)

Orange (bell peppers, pumpkin, carrots, oranges, sweet potatoes)

Green (spinach, kale, broccoli, asparagus, green beans)

Red (radishes, red tomatoes, red peppers, watermelon, guava, beets)

Blue/Purple/Black (blueberries, blackberries, plums, purple cabbage, eggplant)

White (turnips, cauliflower, daikon radish, parsnips, leeks, garlic)

Awareness is the key to finding a diet that works well for you. Pay attention to how your body responds with different foods.

Food Intolerance

For some unknown reason, food allergies and sensitivities are becoming ever more common. These conditions can wreak havoc on the digestive system, causing leaky gut syndrome, Crohn's disease, colitis, chronic inflammation, and many other disorders.

If you suspect that you are suffering from food sensitivities or allergies, you might consider trying an elimination diet, to weed out foods that could be causing you trouble. A typical elimination diet consists of just white rice and lamb, for individuals are very rarely intolerant to those foods.

An elimination diet should last at least several months. For the first month you eat nothing but known safe foods such as lamb and rice. The reason we eat only lamb and rice for a month is that the digestive system might need that much time to heal from the constant exposure that was causing our issues to begin with. If we add elements to our elimination diet too early, it becomes impossible to figure out what is causing the problem because our body never reached a baseline, a state where it isn't inflamed and over-reactive. Allow the inflammation to subside, which takes about a month, before adding in new foods.

Once you get to a point when you are ready to add in a new food, try it once and wait a few days to determine whether it is causing you any trouble. If you notice within a day or two of eating the new food, that you have sores in your month; your rectum or skin itches; you get pimples or rashes; you get gassy; or your jaw, shoulders, or lower back grow tight, it is a hint that that food is not suitable for you at this time. Omit the food from your diet and wait until the symptoms subside before adding another food into the mix.

For most people, it takes many months before they are able to map out what works well for them and what does not. The time it takes to map out your food in this way pays dividends in the long run, though, because with less inflammation, we experience less anxiety, more energy, and more clarity — a better quality of life.

Before starting any new diet, you would be wise to consult your health practitioner.

Chapter 19

Overcoming Perceptual Biases

As human beings we suffer from a number of unconscious biases that can greatly distort our perception of ourselves, others, society, and the world. Generally speaking, we suffer from three primary categories of bias: instinctive negativity bias, emotional bias, and value bias. To improve the quality of our lives, we are wise to become aware of these biases and how they affect our perceptions and reactions.

Instinctive Negativity Bias

The human being has an unconscious bias toward negative awareness, which is to say we are much more motivated to avoid a loss than we are motivated to gain something. As an author, for example, I know that an awful reader experience will garner me a much higher number of negative reviews than will a wonderful reader experience generate positive reviews. Simply put, people are more motivated to express negativity than to express positivity.

Psychological studies have shown time and again that we fear losing money much more than we enjoy gaining it, and so people tend to be much quicker to take actions that prevent a loss than to take a risk that could result in a gain. For this reason, entrepreneurs tend to be a rare breed.

This instinctive negativity bias can be explained by the evolutionary process, which rewards survival of the fittest. From a survival perspective, it is more important to look for danger than it is to pay attention to a possible bounty. Landing a honeycomb is psychologically impactful, but it pales in comparison to being attacked by a tiger.

Although instinctive negativity bias is a vital survival tool, if it remains an unconscious process, we are doomed to miss out on incredible opportunities for life enrichment. The bias will tend to keep us on the tried and true path, which simply means the path we are comfortable with -- which typically is the one that has been limiting us. The meditation process, by its very nature, requires challenging the instinctive negativity bias, so that we can improve our lives with the light of clarity.

Start to notice how you will fight harder not to lose something precious than you will to gain something beneficial. There may be times when losing something is necessary for you to gain something more important. For example, you may find through your meditation process that you are tired of your career and feel inspired to take the risk to do something else with your life. If the negativity bias has its say, you may tamp down your dreams and choose the safe route, only to end up in midlife crisis years later.

Emotional Bias

Alongside the tendency to prioritize negativity over positivity, people also engage in emotional bias, which complicates matters even more. If, for example, we are in a very positive emotional state, such as when someone tells us something we really want to hear, we tend to notice only the positive things around us and overlook negativity. But if we are in a very negative emotional state, we hyperfocus on whatever is perceived as negative around us, no matter how trivial, and tend to miss anything that could be perceived as positive.

Psychologist Paul Eckman described this mood bias in his book *Emotions Revealed* as the emotional refractory period (ERP).

An easy way to understand the phenomenon, according to Dr. Eckman, is to recall a time when you were conversing with someone who said something that threw you off balance. You might recall not having been able to recover quickly enough to respond graciously to the person.

When we are in the emotional refractory period, there is a phase when we are gripped by emotion, which causes our emotional filters to focus on whatever fits with our current emotion.

People who are in love, for example, are typically unable to see the shortcomings or failings of their lovers. Another example is when you are inspired to buy a new car — how your mind is likely to justify to you all the great things about that car while glossing over its negatives.

Many arguments grow heated because of ERP, for during this emotionally fraught time, you may be unable to see anything but the negative in the other person. Suddenly your memory picks out everything they have ever done wrong, to the exclusion of the great things that they might have done. While experiencing ERP, if asked to find positive traits of someone we are angry with, we might find it a monumental struggle to come up with even one good thing to say.

In effect, we are temporarily insane at this time, for information and intelligence that is normally available to use becomes temporarily out of reach. Once past the emotional refractory period, we find that we can easily think of points that would have helped our argument but never occurred to us during it because our intelligence was severely dampened by intense emotionality.

Regardless of whether we are in a positive ERP or a negative ERP, in either case we are seeing the world through emotional filters that limit our clarity. The emotional refractory period is an entirely unconscious response that indicates we are completely out of touch with awareness.

ERP moments can arrive in a flash, without warning, if we are in a beta wave state. They will hit you like a tsunami as your emotions take over and start wreaking havoc with your relationships and your life. Many of the greatest mistakes that we make in our lives are a result of collapsing into the highly emotional, awareness-suppressing ERP.

If we feed such unconscious states by justifying them, falling prey to that sort of unconsciousness becomes easier. The trick to freeing the brain of ERP is to never justify these episodes after they have passed. Yes, ERP is still likely to affect you from time to time, but do not give excuses for it. Instead, admit, at least to yourself, that you fell into a deeply unconscious emotional state and were temporarily insane for a time. Thereafter, as soon as you can, meditate yourself back into a state of conscious awareness.

Vagal breathing works well in such intensely emotional moments. If you find yourself getting triggered, the wise thing to do is to step away from the situation for a lengthy time to make the shift to alpha wave. Understand that getting angry is not going to create a positive result. And forgive yourself when you forget that point.

When we find someone else is in ERP, the tendency will be to try to argue with them or show them how their perception is incorrect by providing counterevidence. This strategy is sure to fail, because the individual is no longer capable of accessing intelligence to see the value of your counterargument. Instead of acknowledging their mistake, they will only see that you are making them look wrong and become even further enflamed. People in ERP are probably incapable of acknowledging that they might be mistaken.

Essentially, when we are in emotional states, we are seeing the world through the filter of our feelings, which means that we are not capable of seeing anything other than what we want to see in that moment.

If you are aware enough to notice that you are in ERP, Dr. Eckman suggests the following: "First, if it's a negatively charged ERP it's better to not talk to anyone or make any decisions. These are the things we say or do that we regret later. Take some time off. Once you feel like you have cooled down and can think straight, you can go back into evaluating the situation." Eckman also advises you to tell others that you will get back to them. He offers the same advice whether we are in a negative or positive state of ERP.

The cause of ERP is always found in the past, via old, unresolved feelings. These unresolved feelings stimulate mental narratives that distort our perception of reality, making us impervious to the truth of what is happening around us and within us.

Dr. Eckman found that the longer the duration of the emotional refractory period, the greater the distortion of reality and the more extensive is the impact on our lives. According to Eckman, a person who remains in ERP for a few days will have a permanently distorted perception of reality related to the events and people perceived to have triggered the ERP. Eckman suggests that correcting episodes of ERP as soon as possible is the best way to curtail any possible lasting negative effects.

Again, once you notice that you have been in ERP, there is no need to blame yourself, for it can happen to anyone. Instead of blame, it is best to calm yourself and go into a state of meditation, so that you can honestly evaluate the perceptions that you had during ERP.

The dangers of ERP affect not only individuals but entire nations. When Barack Obama became president, many on the left were so enamored with him that they could not see any mistakes that he might have made. Many on the right tended to see nothing but the negative, failing to admit when he might have done anything beneficial for the country.

Similarly, when Donald Trump took office, the emotional bias became even more extreme. To many on the Left, Trump is the Devil. To many on the right, he is the Savior. The emotional distortions are likely to have lasting, real-world impacts for decades to come as the sides polarize ever further in their biases and the resulting rhetoric and actions.

The way to have a powerfully transparent political system is to have powerfully transparent individuals, who are no longer so easily manipulated by the emotional patterns of their past.

Value Bias

We have another bias that causes collapse of awareness, much in the way emotional bias stimulated by ERP does. That bias relates to our highest values.

Each individual has a hierarchical set of values that determines, to a large extent, how they see and judge the reality around them. Most people assume that they have chosen their value hierarchy, but in reality the value hierarchy is largely unconscious. It stems from the momentum of the past expressing through us via genetics, personality, childhood influences, culture and ideologies we embraced without question, trauma, and other stuck emotional energies. All of these forces converge to construct the hierarchy of unconscious values that governs our lives.

Becoming aware of your highest unconscious value is vital to improving your quality of life. Whatever yours may be, it is the most dominant, motivating inner force.

The key to discovering the highest of your values is to note which one, when pressured by other values, wins out. For example, if we are willing to lie for money, then we know that wealth or social status takes higher priority in your unconscious value pyramid than does being honest. Many people say that honesty is their highest value, but in truth, there are very few individuals for whom honesty is actually their highest value. Most people will be dishonest to be kind, for example, which shows that kindness has more power within the individual than honesty. Some of those people who are being dishonest to be kind are not as motivated to be kind as much as they are trying to be liked, which means they don't actually value kindness as much as they value approval. For that individual, approval might be the highest of values, followed by kindness, followed by honesty, yet they are likely to think of kindness as their highest.

Kindness provides a great example of how unconscious value bias works. A common spiritual teaching in many traditions is that kindness should be the highest value. Considering the prevalence of this ideology, it provides a great example of the trappings of unconscious bias. No matter how noble a value may seem at first glance, there is always a contradiction, a trap that pulls you out of awareness and creates hypocritical moments when you are unconsciously contradicting your highest value.

If kindness is our highest value, when we meet someone whom we perceive as being kind, we tend to see only the positive and overlook areas where they have character flaws, similar to what happens with ERP.

However, when someone is perceived as being extremely unkind, we tend to overlook everything that they have done right and notice only what they have done wrong. We may go so far as to actively deny anything that they may have done right. At such moments of bias, whether positive or negative, there can be no awareness, because the brain is clearly in the beta wave state of selective attention.

No matter how intelligent we may be as individuals, unless we are highly aware, our emotional state carries more force than does our intelligence, because emotions come from a deeper, older brain than does our rational mind, which is the newest of brain developments. The older the brain structure, the more influence it has over the organism.

Emotions are held in the limbic system, as are motivations and memory. If we have a value bias that places kindness, for example, as our highest value, then we are likely to become emotionally triggered when we perceive someone as not being kind. When this emotional triggering occurs, we can cease being kind, for we may become aggressive as an empathetic response to the one who is perceived as not being kind. In that instance, we are unconsciously betraying our own highest value.

It matters not what our highest value is, for they all have the same pitfall. Your highest value is your judge. It is also the judge of the world. When the highest value is defied, consciously or unconsciously, our emotional response blinds us to reality, and we behave as hypocrites.

So long as we have a specific highest value, we will judge in favor of individuals who seem to fit with that value and against those who seem to be out of sync with it.

A common value of a narcissistic individual is capability. When capability is our highest value, we are prone to condemn those who are less capable as being losers or the dregs of society. Ironically, we will tend to notice the areas where we are quite capable, but overlook areas where we are not strong. Hidden in the value itself is a bias toward what we personally are good at, what our group excels at, or what our nation does well. We will be largely blind to areas where we are not up to snuff.

No one can be good at everything, for we all have weaknesses. Thus, capability as a highest value fails, too. Each value has strength and inherent weakness that leads to hypocrisy.

Only one value does not produce hypocrisy: conscious awareness. It sees all without condemnation. All other highest values are the unconscious momentum of the ages, expressing through us and creating havoc with their influence.

Embrace conscious awareness and be free of the past.

Final Thoughts on Perceptual Biases

Notice how you may have a tendency to negatively speculate about the motives of other people who appear to have done you wrong. These negative speculations about others can happen in a flash. For instance, you might be driving along the road and have someone cut you off or drive past a stop sign out of turn. In that instant, your mind might be saying something bad about that person or their motivations. When that happens, pause and note that you have not always been a perfect driver. Recall that others have probably falsely accused you of motivations that did not reflect your reality. Maybe you accidentally went through a four way stop out of turn, absent any intention to cheat. Remind yourself that you have no way of knowing what the other person's situation is unless they have explicitly told you about their situation and motivation.

Instead of automatically projecting negativity onto other people, see if you can come up with some gracious explanations for why they did what they did — but do so knowing that even those gracious reasons are speculation. The point of the exercise is only to create more flexibility in your brain, so that it is no longer projecting negative motivations by default. Regardless of whether the speculation is positive or negative, there is no need to believe it to be absolutely true.

Finally, make an effort to share something positive in the world. Be thankful. Be uplifting. Be generous. Those actions are extremely healthy for your brain, for other people, and for the world.

Chapter 20

Guiding Emotions

You may be surprised by this fact about your brain, but a great percentage of the cerebral cortex inhibits awareness, to screen out information that we have, consciously or unconsciously, deemed of less importance. This screening is necessary for several reasons. First, what we might call our waking window of perception has a limited data bandwidth. Accordingly, the brain must prioritize which information makes its way into our waking window of perception to let the body have enough information for a chance at survival.

Effectively, the brain inhibits most information from penetrating our awareness. Although the screening is necessary, the process can go awry, depending upon how we prioritize our attention. When priorities are out of balance, our awareness wanes and our lives also fall out of balance.

Once, while I was living in Japan, I had the pleasure of visiting the home of a friend who lived only feet away from the commuter train tracks. I remember having dinner with his family and experiencing a minor earthquake every five minutes as the train passed. The sound was overwhelming, and, to me, extremely distracting.

I asked my friend how he could live so close to the tracks. To my surprise he said that he hardly noticed when the trains passed anymore.

"Doesn't the noise and vibration keep you awake at night?" I asked incredulously.

"No, not really. It bothered me a lot for the first few weeks, but after that, I stopped noticing it. If I focus on it, of course, I will feel it just like you do, but it's no longer a distraction. We just got used to it."

My friend's brain had done an excellent job of screening out information that was deemed to be unhelpful. Consider your heartbeat. Most people are completely unable to feel their heartbeat unless it is racing or they have some sort of heart issue that would make the sensation obvious to them.

You might be surprised to discover that by prioritizing it with our attention, over time, we can become aware of the pulse in the body. You can become aware of your pulse anywhere in the body, at any time. It's amazing to clearly feel its dance everywhere.

The question is, why aren't all of us able to feel our pulse? It's actually not a difficult thing to detect, for your body is being physically moved by the force of those pulses. The only barrier to our awareness is the unconscious filter.

You might not be interested in feeling your pulse, and that is fine, but your brain filters out other pieces of information that you would be wise to notice, such as that state when you are about to be triggered emotionally.

For any emotion to express, the body must be in a posture that is compatible with that emotion. To get an understanding of how emotions express, we can use a wordplay on the term emotion by thinking of its E as meaning energy. E-motion then means "the energy of motion."

All movement is fueled by emotion. If you had absolutely no emotion, you could not move your body, nor could you think, for there would be no fuel for those movements.

When learning to track animals, to understand how tracks are made, a valuable experiment could be made if you bury your body, up to the neck, in the sand and then have people walk around you, so you can feel the pressure releases from their weight shifting on the surface of the sand. Those releases cause waves of pressure to move away from each footfall in every direction through the soil, which you can feel when you are buried in the sand.

If we explore our emotions while being literally buried, we might notice some odd limitations. Humor provides a perfect example of how our bodies are required to move to feel emotion. For example, when buried up to the neck, you might be shocked to discover that you are unable to laugh. Someone could tell you a joke that would have you in stitches normally, but that does not even garner a small chuckle when your body is mostly interred. Not only do you not laugh, you will not feel the least bit of humor.

Not being able to laugh while buried is a completely thought provoking experience. We do not feel humor in such a state because the sand or soil presses into the diaphragm, limiting its movement. Laughter comes from the diaphragm, so if it is unable to move in a way that allows for laughter, not only will we not laugh, we will not even feel humor. The joke, no matter how funny to other people, will elicit no emotional response from you, which means you will feel utterly indifferent to it. Emotion is always tied to motion, and if motion is limited in ways that would curtail the physical expression of a certain emotion, we will not feel that emotion.

Armed with this knowledge, plus the awareness of body positions and how they affect emotions, we can amplify certain feelings of our choosing and curtail other, less healthy emotional patterns.

To possess such a transformative ability, we must first prioritize information that the brain has been blocking from our daily window of perception. We must be interested and paying attention to our body's posture when we feel different emotions. Furthermore, we should notice how those emotions affect our breathing pattern, for each emotion is matched by specific breathing. By changing our posture and breathing consciously, we can have tremendous control over what we feel emotionally and the thoughts that we experience.

We can use our heightened state of awareness to begin mapping our emotions to our body posture and breathing patterns each day. Doing so, we will soon discover that we have power over our emotions through our awareness, posture, and breathing.

Try this exercise: recall a time when you felt tremendous joy. Allow the feelings of joy to take over your body, and once you feel that joy physically, notice your posture, head position, and your breathing pattern. Do the same exercise with a negative emotion, such as sadness. Recall a time when you were utterly crushed with sorrow. Feel that sorrow throughout your body, then notice your posture. You will find that the posture of joy is very different from the posture of sorrow.

Simply by taking on the posture of joy, you will discover that, within a minute or two, you will begin to feel more joyful. Conversely, taking on the posture of sorrow will create feelings of sadness within a few minutes.

Just as there is a breathing range and a posture range for every emotion, so too is there a breathing and posture range related to spherical awareness. To map out the breathing and posture related to spherical awareness, get into a good spherical awareness meditation by following the steps of the Warrior's Meditation. Once you feel spherically expansive, notice the conditions of your body.

- How are you sitting or standing?
- What is your breathing pattern?
- How much physical tension is there?

Practicing to take note of our emotions, thinking, feeling, and how those things relate to body posture and breathing makes us highly aware individuals who are able to constructively guide our subconscious mind. Through such awareness and ability, we are easily able to rewrite our neurology in constructive ways.

Chapter 21

Instant Meditation

After you have been practicing the Warrior's Meditation daily for a month or so, the next step is to start reducing the time spent in each step of the meditation process, so that you can develop the capacity to get into a meditative state more rapidly. With the ability to meditate quickly, expansive awareness will be more easily applied during your day.

Of course, the two-second meditation criterion set by my dojo's tradition is impossible if we are going to go through all seven steps of the basic TEM practice, but note that I am not suggesting those seven steps are not vital in ultimately leading us to the two-second ability. Setting martial arts aside, what is the necessity for being able to achieve a state of meditation in less than two seconds? Considering our modern, high-paced society, and the growing epidemic of anxiety disorders and depression, I suggest that the ability to get in touch with calm, clear being instantly has never been more necessary.

So, how do we train our brains to shift from beta to alpha wave states in an instant? The trick is to gradually reduce the time we allocate to each step in the meditation as we practice over time. There are seven steps to the Warrior's Meditation, if we include vagal breathing in the process. If we practice for 15 minutes each day, as beginners, we are spending about two minutes on each, which is a great time to start with.

To work toward faster meditative abilities, use a timer that you will set to one minute. For each step in the Warrior's Meditation, we will allocate only a minute, which will get us to the last step of expanded awareness about halfway through the practice. Once you get to that final step, remain in that expanded state for the remainder of the time.

What you are likely to discover is that you are able to get into a deeply meditative state in just seven minutes. If that is the case, then reduce the time between each step even further to, say, 30 seconds. What most people discover is that, even with only 30 seconds between each step, they are able to get into just as deep a meditation as they would had they allocated two minutes to each step.

Keep reducing the times between the steps until you start feeling challenged. If you are practicing the Warrior's Meditation each day for 15 minutes, I would bet that within two months, you will be able to do each step in 10 seconds and still reach a powerful meditative state.

Once you get to the stage of achieving a powerful meditation with just five seconds per step, then you are ready to take the leap into instant meditation.

Flash Meditation

The process of flash meditation is simple. First, take a few seconds to assess your degree of inner turmoil. If we were to rank turmoil on a scale from one to ten, where would you fall on the scale in this instant? Be careful to include excitement in your assessment, for excitement is an energy that causes stress because it brings us into beta wave. Even though excitement seems fun, it can rapidly take over and lead to unconscious reactivity.

153

Generally speaking, a rating of four or higher on the turmoil scale would indicate a high potential for unconscious reactivity, because once the energy of turmoil gets that high, it can leap up to a ten in an instant. A rating of three takes a little more time to ramp up into a state of apparent disharmony. With a level of two, it takes quite a bit more time to jump into a reactive state. And with a level of one, you are almost unperturbed. At that level, it will take you a certain amount of effort and time to get riled up. As you practice inner assessment, you become better able to recognize your personal scale, so do not worry too much about any initial vagueness or lack of accuracy in the assessment phase.

Once you have an assessment, give yourself no more than a second or two to flash to the final step of the Warrior's Meditation, which is relaxed spherical awareness. Done properly, the feeling within us and the space around us will seems to calm quite a bit, and our breathing, blood pressure, and even heart rate may slow. As far as our scale goes, we are aiming for a level two or lower during our flash meditations, for at that level we have a much greater chance of remaining more calm throughout our day.

Be careful not to overthink flash meditation. Use your imagination productively to feel the expansion far beyond the body.

As you practice flash meditation regularly for a period of weeks or months, you should notice improvement in your assessments and the depth of calm clarity that you achieve. The entire process of flash meditation should not take longer than five or ten seconds initially. With practice, you will always be aware of any inner turmoil, and you can then skip the turmoil rating and go straight to spherical awareness at any moment.

For the purposes of integrating meditation into daily life, flash meditation is indispensable. As you acclimate to flash meditation, you are likely find that the field of conscious awareness rarely leaves you entirely. You might feel that even when you are focused, somewhere in the background the sense of expansive awareness remains. You will then be able to "foreground" and "background" consciousness, much as you do with windows on your computer. The windows of mind and consciousness then become perspectives between which you can shift back and forth with ease, according to the circumstances. At that stage, the habitual mind is no longer the master.

Setting up a Trigger

Timepieces such as clocks, watches, et cetera can be quite useful triggers. The only problem with timepieces is that, for most of us, they are smartphones. After much experimentation, I have discovered that smartphones are the anathema of conscious awareness for most people.

Thanks to the extensive dopamine addictions that many of us have fostered with our smartphones, we tend to collapse out of meditation merely by glancing at one. Even for advanced meditators, smartphones can prove to be a nemesis. Keep in mind, though, that our failures are really lessons and challenges to overcome. That said, a smartphone may be too challenging early on. For individuals who are not addicted to their smartphones, they might work as a great trigger. For anyone with smartphone issues, however, it is wise initially to choose a different trigger.

The key to setting up a good trigger depends upon how often we consciously access that trigger. A bad trigger might be a painting in our office that we unconsciously look at while taking a break every now and again throughout the day. Because we are not interacting with the painting with conscious intent, it may not have enough power to remind us to flash meditate. Choose something that you interact with intentionally. Clocks are great that way, precisely because we look at them only with purpose. We want to be practicing flash meditation at least five to ten times per day, so whatever it is that you choose should be something you encounter with purpose at least that many times every day.

Once you decide upon a trigger, you'll need to empower that trigger. The way to empower it is to run through the flash meditation process with it repeatedly, at least five times, back to back. Look at the trigger, flash into relaxed spherical awareness, and then look away. Then look at it again and flash again into relaxed spherical awareness. Repeat three more times, and you are likely to have established a functional trigger.

The way to test that trigger is to go about your day without further conscious thought of flash meditation. If the next time you interact with your designated stimulus, it reminds you to flash meditate, then you know the trigger is well set. If it fails to remind you to meditate, either the trigger was not set well or, because of your lack of purposeful interaction with the object, it is not a good triggering device.

Warning: each time that your chosen object reminds you to meditate and you choose not to meditate, you are weakening the trigger. To keep the trigger strong, we need to keep reinforcing the association between it and the action of flash meditating.

Chapter 22

Returning to Essentials

Now that we have learned multiple, flexible applications and uses for the Warrior's Meditation, it is important to remind the reader that all good training rests on a solid foundation of fundamentals. My martial arts teacher in Japan — Shizen Osaki, a master instructor of multiple samurai arts — often says that the secret to mastery is found in the basics. Of course, when I entered the tradition and began my studies, I was eager to move through the basics to explore the more tantalizing advanced techniques. I found it odd that my teacher kept reminding even senior students to pay attention to the basics. But after receiving the Master's License and becoming a teacher myself, I too have noticed people's tendency to skim over the basics and, in doing so, miss vital elements that cause them to struggle more than they would otherwise.

With regard to the basics, meditation is just like the martial arts — glossing over fundamentals is certain to lead to otherwise unnecessary struggle and potentially prevent mastery. Much like the way my teacher often reminded me, I also encourage my students to return to the basics for refinement when they hit a seemingly impenetrable barrier in their meditation practice. In my own studies, I return to the basics repeatedly, and I believe doing so has proved tremendously beneficial to my life.

With regard to mediation, not only do we tend to underestimate the importance of the basics, but we also tend to associate the practice with strict discipline, an association that causes its own set of problems over time. Associating meditation with discipline is totally understandable, considering that many of the ancient traditions from which modern meditation derives teach that strict discipline is necessary for meditation. Unfortunately, strict discipline can lead to rigidity and create unnecessary effort, which is actually counterproductive in meditation.

Furthermore, it is a common teaching worldwide that anything worth doing takes a lot of effort. Movies, TV, and of course sports glorify victory through blood, sweat, and tears, so children and adults alike fantasize about fighting through unbeatable odds to come out the other side, victorious. Surely these fantasies run deep into our genetic past, when life was not so easy and fighting tooth and nail for survival was sometimes a requirement.

I have spent the majority of my life training in ancient Japanese traditions. Through that training, I discovered a strange dichotomy with regard to discipline, for the teachers could be quite harsh about that aspect, yet they would, through kuden (oral traditions taught at higher levels) insist that the true path was one of effortless effort and nonresistance.

Through my own practice, I have discovered that a truly transformative meditation is a joyful experience of connectedness with the deepest inner being and the environment around us. I found that developing a healthy, powerful meditation practice does not require strict discipline (although a certain amount of discipline is appropriate), but it does take persistence and right attitude toward practice.

Regarding persistence, what I am referring to is best modeled by a toddler learning to walk. The toddler has no concept of discipline. Instead, it has a strong instinctive desire to walk that stimulates it to try again and again regardless of past failures and painful landings. The toddler falls over and over, sometimes crying in frustration, but before long it is attempting to stand yet again. Usually, through natural persistence, the individual is eventually able to walk, run, and ultimately develop the capacity to do all the things that healthy adults take for granted.

Much in the way a toddler learns to walk through persistence, we must be persistent in establishing a meditation practice within our daily lives. Eventually, through daily engagement, there will be so much momentum in our meditation practice that it will seem as if the universe itself is meditating through our bodies. That is The Way.

Over the years I have received a steady stream of questions regarding the Total Embodiment Method. Whether from beginners or long-time meditators, most of these questions have a common theme and could be answered in a similar way: "Show up to your meditation practices daily, but during practice use progressively less effort — relax."

The only question concerns how we, as busy students, parents, employees, and bosses make time for daily meditation. Unless we take the time to practice meditation every day, we will be unable to gain its benefits.

Thanks to the functional flexibility of TEM, I believe you will find it quite easy to fit into your daily schedule. You can practice on the fly, in the midst of your daily life — in the car, while walking, while talking, while working. With regular sustained practice of the basics, awareness will enrich your life and the lives of people around you. Your spouse, your children, your friends, and even your boss will be better off because of your time spent embodying awareness.

Keep it simple and stick with it daily — your life will improve.

Chapter 23

Natural Meditation

In the mid-2000s, I met with a well-known survival instructor in Japan, who had learned from first nation lineages. I had been living in Tokyo since the late 1990s to study traditional martial and healing arts. Although survival skills are no longer taught in Japanese martial arts schools, in the days of the Samurai, it was a part of the curriculum, so I was taking survival courses to supplement my martial arts training.

The instructor knew that I was an advanced martial artist and an avid meditator, so he asked me about my meditation method. He listened carefully as I explained my basic approach. Then he said, "Who taught you that meditation? That's a secret method taught only at the highest levels."

The question caught me a little off guard because the method I was using seemed to be so natural and beneficial that it couldn't and shouldn't be a secret. Admittedly, the method is distinctive compared to other meditations born of Eastern religions and spiritual systems, but secret?

I told him that I thought the method was very straightforward and basic, but he again stressed that the meditation was actually the most advanced.

His comments stuck in the recesses of my mind for years. During that time, I didn't share the method with anyone other than Osaki Sensei. I didn't find ease of mind about sharing the method outside my teacher's dojo until some years later, when it was my responsibility to teach.

Upon my return to the United States, I immediately opened a dojo and began teaching. Because of my concerns about the meditation method, I held off sharing it for more than a year. Although I sometimes talked about meditation after class, I didn't think my students were particularly interested in it. To my surprise, one day, one of the students asked me to teach meditation.

Initially I felt hesitation because of the doubts I harbored. I worried that the meditation method might be too difficult for my students. Considering that the floor above our dojo was a noisy dance studio, I also felt concerned that the racket would be overly distracting.

With the lack of insulation between our ceiling and their hardwood floors, the divider became a giant speaker, amplifying the music and the footfalls. The intense vibrations constantly shook the ceiling tiles, causing little white particles to flutter down onto the black training mats.

Considering the racket, I couldn't imagine beginners meditating there. In spite of the obstacles, the requests for a meditation lesson continued.

Eventually I decided to try. The music was blaring, as usual, and vibrations from the dancers' feet hitting the floor sounded like a buffalo ballet, but my students were eager. To my great surprise they entered into a powerful meditative state in the midst of the racket.

We meditated for about 20 minutes before beginning martial arts practice. To the students' delight, once they began martial arts training, they discovered that the meditation had greatly improved their execution of martial techniques.

About a month later another instructor who was sharing space with me asked if his six-year-old son could join the meditation portion of the lesson. Initially I assumed that a child could not meditate, but because the boy really seemed sincere, I let him try. I figured I could let him leave the lesson early if he appeared bored.

To my astonishment, the boy was perfectly suited to the meditative experience. He appeared to love meditating; this impression was confirmed when he eagerly asked if he could join the next lesson.

In light of the child's incredible success, I began teaching meditation more openly. I felt that these experiences demonstrated the suitability of the method for beginner and advanced meditators alike. My conclusion: TEM is not advanced; it's natural.

I began to wonder, though, why the method was all but unknown to the world. After all, it seemed totally obvious to me. Considering the subject for a time and reflecting upon how I discovered it, I concluded that the method is so natural that it has simply been overlooked, for we often fail to notice the simplest things.

I began to speculate that modern teachers do not know this method because it was rarely, if ever, taught explicitly, for there was no need. In the old days, over the course of a disciple's advancement, the incorporation of the principles of awareness would occur quite naturally.

In India, for example, advanced meditators usually spent weeks, months, or even years living as ascetics in the wild as a part of their training. During their time alone in the wilderness, the adept naturally acquired the essence of the TEM method without ever having been taught it. The same would have been true of hunter-gatherers around the world, regardless of the era in which they lived.

I surmised that under those primal circumstances, there was never a need to formulate a method. Simply put, if a human being is placed in the right environmental context, alone, for a sufficient length of time, an expansive meditative awareness emerges automatically.

Imagine living alone in the jungles of India, where leopards, cobras, and all manner of possibly gruesome death might seek you out. Under such circumstances, a certain calm, expansive awareness necessarily emerges that simultaneously conserves your energy, enhances instinct, and lends a sense of oneness with the environment. Without these vital qualities you would probably die from anxiety-fueled blunders or be eaten.

The key to bringing out these qualities resides in the natural beauty of the environment, as well as the dangers and pressures of living off the land.

Absent the influence of nature or not having a well-articulated method to bring out our innate awareness, we begin to rely on contrived methods that take more effort and that are, to some degree, inconsistent with the survival requirements of living in the wild.

I understood that TEM, although my formulation, is just a way to simulate what occurs naturally when human beings are in the right circumstances. From that perspective, TEM does not represent a new meditation method but, instead, the original, primal meditation. Because TEM is totally natural, it can never be truly lost to the world, for so long as there are humans living in the wilderness, it will tend to emerge spontaneously, even if those humans are not able to articulate the meditation.

Long-term dedication to natural meditation has proved invaluable to my own personal transformation in daily life, allowing for a deeply integrated embodiment of awareness. I have also found natural awareness to be transformative in many other areas of study, including healing modalities, martial arts, and, of course, survival skills. After years of teaching TEM, I have realized that it blends well with each of our lives in unique but overlapping ways and stimulates a profound transformation within the individual that then shines into the world.

To give credit where it is due for the development of TEM, Samurai training, healing work, and vision questing have been the most obvious contributors to the method.

TEM opens the senses, heightens awareness, and integrates us by bringing about a sense of inner peace and unity. Most importantly, it helps us to embody awareness, taking us out of realms of mental abstraction, philosophy, and ego and into a sustained, lived experience of the present moment.

Maybe when we lived close to the earth, humans had no need to formulate a meditation to be aware and feel unified, but now that so few of us live nature-centric lives, and so many of us feel disconnected, we have a real need to reconnect with life, and for that we need the power of natural methods such as TEM.

So, what is it that makes modern humans so unaware and out of touch? From early childhood we are taught to focus through all that we do. Children are unconsciously trained to focus their attention to exclusion through chatting, watching TV, surfing the Internet, playing video games, reading, writing, et cetera. Few common activities, if any, bring out the kind of relaxed awareness like that of a Samurai master or an Amazonian shaman, for example.

The effect of habitual focus is psychological disharmony, which can stimulate self-centeredness, anxiety, depression, and any number of other maladies born of a sense of separation from the world around us.

Fortunately, we don't need to join a tribe or live alone in the wilderness to find a sense of connection. We can access it in our homes, on the train, in our cars, at work, and ultimately throughout our daily lives, once we acclimate to the practice.

Because TEM represents the first and most natural approach to meditation that is in alignment with our evolutionary development, it is perfectly suited to aid modern humans in rebalancing perception, re-establishing the natural sense of unity, and cleaning up the inner space so that distrust, unreasonable fear, anxiety, depression, and self-centeredness have no abode. Practicing these natural methods will move us ever toward vibrant inspiration and clarity.

The only question remaining is, are you ready to elevate awareness in your life?

If you would like support in your meditation practice, we can practice together. Visit the link below to gain complimentary access to 30-days of my daily guided meditation service.
www.richardlhaight.com/services

Thank you so much for reading *The Warrior's Meditation*. If you enjoyed the book, please consider leaving a review at Amazon.com. Thank you!

To receive notifications of future book, video, and course publications by Richard L. Haight, visit, www.richardlhaight.com/notifications

Ready Reference

MANTRA

Numerous traditional meditation approaches make use of mantra, but the most popular is probably Transcendental Meditation, commonly known as TM. TM got much of its early popularity from the Beatles, who were vocal practitioners and ardent supporters of Maharishi Mahesh Yogi, the founder of TM.

Maharishi Mahesh Yogi formulated TM — a school of Samatha concentration meditation — in India, in the early 20th century. As TM is a concentration method, there is a prescribed point of focus. The focal point of TM is on the repeating of a mantra in your mind, which is practiced for 20 minutes, twice a day, with eyes closed.

Although practitioners say that TM is not a religious practice, detractors argue that the use of a mantra is a religious element. In fact, in 1977, thanks to the perceived religious nature of the TM method, a U.S. federal district court ruled that a curriculum in TM that was being taught in some New Jersey schools was in violation of the First Amendment.

Whether religious or secular in nature, TM has spread throughout the world and is even practiced in some schools and prisons, with many people claiming benefit from the practice.

To get an idea of how mantra works, I have summarized a basic secular approach that you can practice.

Time

For your initial practice, 15 minutes is good.

Place

Any comfortable place without distraction.

Position

Sit comfortably with your spine lightly erect.

Eyes

Closed

Process

Close your eyes, and use your breath to relax the body. Just a few deep breaths are generally sufficient to settle the body, but take as many as you need to accomplish relaxation.

During the 15-minute practice, repeat a mantra in your mind. A mantra is typically a one-syllable word or short phrase. For your experience, you can use any word that you like. It could be a word in your own language or in another. Select a word that conveys a meaning that you like. For example, you could use a word like "love," "peace," or "one."

Ending Meditation

After 15 minutes, open your eyes and move your fingers and toes for a few minutes to stimulate a rise in your blood pressure before you attempt to stand up. Stand slowly and carefully and go about your day.

Dealing with Distraction

When a thought or inner agitation arises, simply return your attention to the mantra.

Mantra Summary

1. Meditate for 15 minutes
2. Sit comfortably with spine lightly erect and eyes closed
3. Repeat your mantra in your mind (a word such as "love," "peace," or "one")
4. To end meditation, open eyes and move fingers and toes for several minutes to stimulate your blood pressure before standing

ZEN MEDITATION

Zazen, which means "seated Zen," is the primary meditation practice found in Zen Buddhism. Zen is one of the most well-known, yet least understood forms of Buddhism in the world.

Zen is a Japanese form of Mahayana Buddhism. When Buddhism came to China from India, it was quite naturally influenced by Taoist philosophy and became what is known as the Chan School of Buddhism, which is somewhat distinct from Indian Buddhism.

Zen meditation, known as Zazen, emphasizes disciplined practice and rigorous self-control, qualities that the Samurai prized. For that reason, Zen is a religion closely tied to many Samurai martial arts systems.

Zen focuses more on direct experiential perception of the nature of reality and living by that insight in daily life for the benefit of society than it does on Sutras (religious teachings of Buddhism). As such, the practice of seated meditation is for the express purpose of attaining insight.

Zen could be looked at as a mix of Samatha and Vipassana, for it embraces concentration (Samatha), but it does so for the express purpose of realizing the essential nature of reality, which is a Vipassana (awareness) aim.

My first Zazen experience was at a famously strict temple in Kamakura, Japan. I was surprised to discover that the Zen master walked around the meditation room with a keisaku, which may be translated as "warning stick," as we sat cross-legged on zabuton (sitting cushions) with our spines perfectly erect and eyes gazing downward, almost closed, at a 45-degree angle. Although I quite enjoyed the practice, the strict nature of Zazen and the potential of getting hit with a stick (even if it causes no actual damage) might put off many people.

Zen masters use keisaku to strike the shoulders of meditators who are slouching or losing concentration. Depending upon the temple, the strikes may occur at the request of the meditator or at the discretion of the master. In either case, the strikes are considered acts of compassion meant to help the meditator, not punishments.

Two main schools of Zen exist in modern Japan. The Rinzai school makes use of koans. Koans are stories, dialogues, questions, or statements used to baffle the mind into silence. The Soto school does not make use of koans but instead emphasizes silent, concentrated meditation to realize "no-mind."

As this book is intended to highlight simple, secular meditation approaches, I will describe the basic meditation method of the Soto school here, for in the translation of koan from Japanese to English, much can be lost in meaning and effect. Koan or not, both schools emphasize the need for concentration. The main difference is found in the specific focal point.

According to the Soto school, proper meditation practice is as follows (I have omitted religious requirements for altars, incense, statues, and/or paintings of religious figures, which are commonly recommended by the school, as we are not necessarily practicing for religious purposes here):

Time

Use a timer and set it for 20 minutes for the first few practice sessions. At the temple where I practiced, I believe we practiced for about an hour, but 20 minutes should be sufficient for most people to get a sense of this meditation method.

Personal Preparation

It is wise to avoid meditating when tired or sleepy. It is also advised to eat moderately and avoid alcohol prior to meditation. To stimulate wakefulness it is a good idea to wash your face and feet with cold water just prior to meditation practice.

Place

Find a quiet, clean place to sit where there will be little chance of disturbance. The place should be comfortably light and warm, not too bright nor too dim, too hot nor too cold.

Clothing

Avoid wearing tight or heavy clothing which might cut off circulation or create pressure on the joints. Wearing socks to keep your feet warm is a good idea.

Cushion

As you will likely not have Zen cushions to sit on, it is recommended to use a small but firm couch pillow to sit on in a carpeted room, placing the base of your spine at the center of the pillow so that half of it is behind you.

Leg Positioning

Although the full-lotus or half-lotus positions are recommended, if you are unable to sit in those positions easily, just cross your legs in a way that is most comfortable to you.

If you are quite flexible and would like to try practicing in the full-lotus position, begin by placing your right foot on your left thigh and then your left foot on your right thigh. The tips of your toes and the outer edge of your thighs should line up.

For most people, the full-lotus is not a comfortable position to sit in, but you may be comfortable in the half-lotus position. To do so, pull your right foot under your left thigh and place your left foot on your right thigh, with the heel at the hip. If you are more flexible with the other leg, you may place your right foot on your left thigh instead, with your left leg crossed under your right thigh. Again, the tips of your toes and the outer edge of your thigh should line up.

Regardless of which position you choose to sit in, aim to cross your legs to form an equilateral triangle from the spine to each knee to balance your body weight equally on those three points.

Posture

Straighten the lower back and spine, while pushing the buttocks outward and the abdomen forward. Extend your neck toward the ceiling and tuck in your chin. The aim should be to have your ears in line with your shoulders and your nose lined up with your navel.

Once in position, relax your shoulders, back, and abdomen as much as you can without visibly changing your posture, while aiming to remain physically centered.

Hand Position

Place both hands, palm-up, with your wrists resting on your inner thighs at your abdomen, with the tips of your thumbs lightly touching each other just in front of your navel. Create a little space between your arms and your body.

The mouth

Keep your mouth closed, placing the tip of your tongue against the roof of your mouth just behind your teeth.

Eyes

Closing your eyes will cause drowsiness or daydreaming, so keep them slightly open while gazing downward at roughly a 45-degree angle.

Breath

At first, slightly open your mouth and take deep, long, smooth breaths with the aim to expel all the air from the bottom of your lungs. After this initial breath, close your mouth and breathe naturally through your nose. There is no need to control your breath or breathe heavily. Just let the breath take on a life of its own.

Awareness

In Soto Zazen practice there is no aim to concentrate on any particular external object, mantra, or to control thought. Instead, your focus should be on maintaining a proper sitting posture. According to Zen, if your posture is right and your breathing settles, your mind will quiet.

Of course, thoughts will likely arise, but the aim is to allow them without interest, avoidance, or struggle. Allow thoughts and feelings to come and go of their own accord. The only concern during Zazen is to remain in proper posture and allow the breath to settle.

Ending Meditation

Getting up after sitting for an extended period of time can be dangerous if your legs have fallen asleep or if your blood pressure has dropped. For this reason, it is wise to move a bit prior to standing up. Sway your body left and right, front and back a few times, at first slightly and then more vigorously, while taking deep breaths. Unfold your legs and stretch them out to allow circulation to return to them. Rise slowly and carefully.

Zen Meditation Summary

1. Set a timer for 20 minutes
2. Eat moderately and avoid alcohol prior to meditation. Wash face and feet to stimulate wakefulness
3. Wear loose fitting, comfortable clothing and socks to keep your feet warm
4. Meditate in a quiet, clean, moderately warm room where there will be little disturbance
5. Sit on cushion and cross legs
6. Straighten the spine and tuck in your chin, then relax your shoulders, back, and abdomen while maintaining an upright posture
7. Hands, palm-up, wrists resting on your inner thighs, with the tips of your thumbs lightly touching each other
8. Close mouth with the tip of your tongue against the roof of your mouth behind your teeth
9. Eyes slightly open and gazing downward at 45-degree angle
10. Initially, take deep, long, smooth inhales with exhales aimed to expel all air from bottom of lungs. Finally, close your mouth and breathe naturally through your nose
11. Focus on maintaining proper posture
12. Allow thoughts and feelings to come and go of their own accord
13. End the meditation by swaying your body left and right, front and back, while taking deep breaths before rising from meditation.

MINDFULNESS MEDITATION

Mindfulness meditation is a Vipassana or awareness approach, and it was the first meditation that I experienced, although I didn't know it was called mindfulness meditation at the time. As I stated in the Introduction, my girlfriend taught it to me when I was 16 years old.

The very first time that I practiced mindfulness meditation was after a having a terrible argument with my mother. I left the house in a rage and hiked up the hill behind our property, with no plan in mind other than to get away for a time.

Once I got to the top of the hill, I felt drawn to sit in a certain spot under a large eucalyptus tree, where I was inspired to try the meditation technique that my girlfriend had taught me just a few days earlier. She never mentioned how she learned this method, but the technique was relatively simple, so I gave it a try.

Although it took quite some time of intense concentration before my inner feeling began to shift, eventually the rage disappeared. Rage was replaced by a profound sense of clarity and connection to the environment around me. I felt totally free.

After this initial experience, I fell in love with meditation and practiced it regularly thereafter, but I could never get back to the magical state of perfect tranquility and connectedness that I had experienced the very first time I employed the method.

The failure to replicate that ideal experience stimulated me to search for a way of meditation that took less effort and more easily integrated with my daily life. That search ultimately led me to Japan and the formation of the Total Embodiment Method.

Although mindfulness meditation is said to have its roots in Vipassana, an Indian Buddhist meditative practice, it is actually a secular meditation popularized by Jon Kabat-Zinn and used as a means of reducing stress and increasing wellness.

In terms of popularity, mindfulness meditation is rivaled only by TM and Zazen meditation. In terms of aim, mindfulness is probably closest in relationship to the Total Embodiment Method, with their common goal of enhancing well-being by sustaining present awareness.

Mindfulness meditation is devoid of Buddhist culture, tradition, and religious teachings. Basically, mindfulness meditation is about paying attention to the present moment and what is actually occurring within us and without while making no attempt to escape from reality as it arises. In my estimation, the aim to be fully present is highly beneficial.

Mindfulness has a recommended approach to the basic meditation practice, which is typically done seated. Here are the basic steps of the seated meditation practice:

Time

Use a timer and set it for at least 15 minutes during the first few practice sessions. I probably did several hours when I was on the hill, but my emotional situation was quite extreme. Fifteen minutes should be sufficient for most people to get a sense of this meditation method, but trust your intuition if it is calling for more time.

Place

If you are comfortable being in nature, it is advisable to try mindfulness meditation outdoors a few times, weather permitting. There is no need to go far into the wild. A local park, your backyard, or somewhere outside where you can find solitude would be fine. If possible, use your intuition to find the location. Absent an outdoor option, a soothing room in your home is the next best thing.

The body is highly influenced by its environment, so meditating to declutter the mind while in a cluttered room is ill-advised. If it is necessary to meditate indoors and there are no uncluttered rooms, it is wise to clean and harmoniously arrange the room that you intend to use before meditating.

Positioning

Sit comfortably wherever you would like to practice, your spine lightly erect but not overly stiff. If you wish to sit in a chair, try to use one that will allow for 90 degree angles at the ankles, knees, and hips, so that the joints do not overextend during the meditation, something that can cause pain and misalignment over time. If available chairs are too short, you can add a cushion to the chair to raise you and accomplish the desired angles. It is advised to keep the bottoms your feet flat on the floor.

If you prefer to sit cross-legged on the floor, it is advisable to prop up the buttocks by placing a cushion under them. If we place our buttocks directly on the floor, we are likely to experience hip, abdominal, and lower-back fatigue that will cause distraction during the meditation and possibly cause discomfort later.

For individuals who are comfortable sitting on the knees Japanese style (seiza), we can take pressure off the knees and ankles and prevent losing circulation to our lower legs by placing a pillow under our buttocks, between our legs. Doing so should make the position quite comfortable for most people and allow the spine to be upright and at ease.

The lotus or half-lotus position is fine for those individuals who can assume it comfortably. If it takes effort or there is any discomfort with the position, it is ill-advised. Individuals who are unaware of the lotus position are probably not conditioned to use it and are advised to avoid it.

Once in the seated position, lightly straighten the spine without being rigid, which means allow the spine's natural curvature. Allow your head to rest comfortably on the neck vertebrae, without stretching the neck upward, the way Zazen advises. Also, allow your arms to be parallel to the sides of your body, with your hands resting comfortably on the thighs, without crossing your arms. The key is to find a comfortable position for your hands so that you can sit for a long period without having to shift positions. If the hands are too far forward, they will pull on the body, causing it to hunch. If the hands are too far back, the shoulders will be jammed up, which will cause stiffness. Balance is the key.

Eyes

Much as in Zazen, tuck in your chin a little and let your gaze fall gently downward at a roughly 45-degree angle. Also like Zazen, close your eyes almost entirely, leaving just enough of an opening that you can still see. If your intuition indicates that you should close your eyes, that is fine. The key with the eyes is to keep them from focusing on anything in particular.

Focal Point

Once you are comfortably seated and relaxed, notice the flow of your relaxed breath. With each inhalation mentally state, "breathing in," and with each exhalation, mentally note, "breathing out."

During mindfulness practice, the mind is sure to wander away from the breath and project various scenes of the future or past, narratives about you or what you are hankering for or disliking. The aim is not to fight or avoid thinking. At some point, your attention will snap out of the thought loop and notice that you were thinking. When that "waking" moment occurs to you, kindly return attention to the breath without any concern over the thoughts or feelings that stole attention for a time.

Adjustments

If you feel the urge to adjust your physical positioning, stretch, or scratch somewhere, that is fine, but take a moment to be aware of the urge before allowing the movement. The moment of awareness will help prevent unconscious movement from taking over. As an alternative to moving, you might decide not to follow the urge, but even in that event, just take note of your pause and your choice.

If the mind rambles on or wanders constantly, have no concern, for that is entirely normal. Just notice that the mind is wandering or rambling without getting upset about it, if possible.

Ending Meditation

Just as with any seated meditation, your blood pressure can drop during the practice, so be sure to move around for a few minutes while seated to ensure that your blood pressure is raised before you stand.

Once you are up and ready for the rest of your day, be sure to pause long enough to notice how your body feels, your environment, and how you would like to spend your day, for noticing is the very essence of mindfulness.

Mindfulness Meditation Summary

1. Sit comfortably, spine lightly erect, head resting comfortably on the vertebrae
2. Eyes are partially closed and aimed downward at a 45-degree angle
3. Breathe through the nose with full, yet relaxed breaths; if nose breathing is uncomfortable, then mouth breathing is fine
4. Notice the breath and mentally note "breathing in" during inhalation and "breathing out" during exhalation
5. When the mind wanders, simply return attention to the breath once you notice the wandering

VAGAL BREATHING

Take in a completely full breath and hold it, while using the breath to stretch the lungs in a way that feels really good. By repositioning your abdomen, spine, shoulders, and neck, you will find that you can move the air pressure around in the lungs.

Play with the pressure in the lungs by stretching them to find which directional pressure feels best for you in the moment. If it feels good to stretch in this way for a few seconds and then shift to another direction, and then another, that is fine. Exhale.

Don't think too much about this process, for with any meditation, feeling is the key to a powerful experience. Here is a link to a video I made that demonstrates vagal breathing:

https://richardllhaight.com/vagal

Stretch the lungs with the pressure of your breaths for as long as it feels good, then exhale in a way that also feels deeply satisfying. Pause and relax for as long as feels good before taking several relaxed recovery breaths as you like. Take another stretching breath as soon as you feel ready to do so. Repeat this breathing process for five minutes.

The key with vagal breathing is not being particularly willful but instead paying attention to what feels good at each stage of the process. If vagal breathing is done properly, which means paying attention to what feels really good, the brain will shift from beta to alpha wave during the first breath. With fifteen minutes of practice, vagal breathing should noticeably drain tension from your body and create a warm, clear, calm feeling.

FIXED-POINT FOCUS

Start a stopwatch and focus completely on a candle flame or a chosen single point on the wall to exclusion. Take note of how long it requires before you can no longer exclude the total visual field. The purpose of this exercise is to become aware of the fact that you can't consciously stop seeing the total visual field, so long as your eyes are open.

PERIPHERAL VIEWING EXERCISE

Sit comfortably for 15 minutes and consciously be attentive to the entire visual field without any attempt to focus or exclude information.

CONSCIOUS HEARING

Set your timer for 5 minutes, close your eyes, relax the body as much as possible, and listen carefully to all sound from all directions, near and far. Make no attempt to identify any sound. Instead, become engrossed in feeling sound. If you relax with this exercise, you will find is that in less than a minute, you are in a powerfully aware state of meditation.

If you find that you are attracted to or annoyed by any specific sound, your serial processing, noisy hemisphere is activated, and you are no longer in a meditative state. Thus, to remain in a meditative state, we simply accept all sounds without bias and without any attempt to identify.

Once the timer goes off, start it again and redo the meditation, this time with your eyes open. At first, your attention might be tempted by the things in your visual field, but in that event, just keep returning your attention to the total auditory field.

CONSCIOUS OLFACTION

Sit comfortably for 15 minutes with your eyes closed and take full smooth breaths with the intention of feeling the quality of the air as it travels through your nostrils, into the lungs, and back out again. Notice the general qualities of the air, including the air pressure, the moisture, and freshness, as well as the overall sense of smell.

Do not get caught up in trying to identify any particular smell, just accept all smells while feeling the air traveling through the nasal passages.

Open your eyes to continue the meditation once you notice the shift to alpha, which is when your mind and body feel calm and relaxed.

Usually by the second time you practice Conscious Olfaction, you can do it easily with your eyes open from the outset.

CONSCIOUS TASTING

Become vibrantly aware of the feeling in the mouth as well as the general sense of taste.

There may be detectible traces of flavors that you consumed earlier in the day, but make no attempt to identify specific tastes. Just be aware of the sense of taste and the feeling in the mouth, as if it were your first time ever experiencing the mouth.

Be careful to notice when the shift to alpha occurs.

CONSCIOUS FEELING

Sit comfortably for 15 minutes, allowing a minute or two between each step.

First, pay vibrant attention to the whole of your feet and consciously relax them.

Next, vibrantly feel the area between your ankles and your knees and consciously relax those areas.

Now, feel the space between your knees and your hips and consciously relax that area.

When you are ready, vibrantly feel the area between your hips and your lower ribcage and relax.

Next, give your attention to the area between your lower ribs and your collar bones and relax the area.

When you feel ready for the next step, pay vibrant attention to the area between your collar bones and the top of your head. Relax it deeply.

Now, feel the space between your collar bones and your elbows. Consciously relax that space.

Next, notice the area between your elbows and your wrists. Relax.

Now, feel your hands and fingers. Especially relax this area.

Finally, pay attention to the total space of your entire body, the inner dimension as well as the surface area, and relax the entire body such that there is just enough tension to remain upright.

SPHERICAL AWARENESS EXERCISE

Imagine a light, pleasant feeling in your chest. Once you get a sense for the feeling, spread it throughout your body. If you find there are areas of the body that seem resistant to this light feeling, you are getting an experience of what I described earlier as heavy areas in my body. Do not try to force those areas to lighten at this time. Just take note of them without focusing on them.

Next, imagine that light, pleasant feeling spreading beyond your body spherically to create a positive atmosphere in the space around you. Be sure that your feeling does not stop at surfaces, but moves right through them. There is no reason walls, floors, or ceilings need limit your intention or awareness, so softly extend your feeling/intention beyond those things.

SUMMARY OF THE WARRIOR'S MEDITATION

1. Take several vagal breaths to relax the body and mind
2. Pay attention to the total visual field
3. Notice all sound, near and far
4. Notice the sense of smell and the feeling in the breathing passages
5. Notice the sense of taste and the feeling in the mouth
6. Notice the feeling of the entire body
7. Expand your feeling spherically beyond the body to the space around you
8. Rise by keeping spatial awareness primary in your attention, move your fingers and toes and lean left and right to be sure your blood pressure returns to a safe level before you stand; stand in awareness

MAPS OF THE MIND

1. Self-image — how we see ourselves
2. Social status — what others expect of us

3. Beliefs — what we believe to be true

FOUR STAGES OF COMPETENCE

1. Unconscious incompetence — wrong intuition
2. Conscious incompetence — wrong analysis
3. Conscious competence — right analysis
4. Unconscious competence — right intuition

THREE PERCEPTUAL BIASES

1. Instinctive Negativity Bias
2. Emotional Bias
3. Value Bias

INSTANT MEDITATION

Take a few seconds to assess your degree of inner turmoil and rate it on a scale from 1 to 10. A rating of 4 or higher on the turmoil scale would indicate a high potential for unconscious reactivity.

Once you have an assessment, give yourself no more than a second or two to flash into spherical awareness. Go about your day and see how long you are able to remain spherically aware.

Sources

Baas L.S. et al. "An Exploratory Study of Body Awareness in Persons
with Heart Failure Treated Medically or with Transplantation." Journal of
Cardiovascular Nursing Vol. 19, Issue 1, Jan-Feb. 2004.
https://www.ncbi.nlm.nih.gov/pubmed/14994780

Bushdid, C. et al. "Humans Can Discriminate More than 1 Trillion
Olfactory Stimuli." Science Vol. 343, 21 Mar. 2014.
http://vosshall.rockefeller.edu/assets/file/BushdidScience2014.pdf

Christensen, A.J. et al. "Body Consciousness, Illness-Related
Impairment, and Patient Adherence in Hemodialysis." Journal of Consulting and
Clinical Psychology Vol. 64, Issue 1, Feb. 1996.
https://www.ncbi.nlm.nih.gov/pubmed/8907094

de Groot, Jasper H. B. et al. "Chemosignals Communicate Human
Emotions." Psychological Science Vol. 23, Issue 11, 27 Sept. 2012.
https://journals.sagepub.com/doi/abs/10.1177/0956797612445317

Eriksson, Elsa M. et al. "Aspects of the non-pharmacological treatment of
irritable bowel syndrome." World J Gastroenterol. 2015 Oct 28. 2015.
https://www.ncbi.nlm.nih.gov/pmc/articles/PMC4616219/

Eriksson, Elsa M. et al. "Aspects of the non-pharmacological treatment of
irritable bowel syndrome." World J Gastroenterol. 2015 Oct 28. 2015.
https://www.ncbi.nlm.nih.gov/pmc/articles/PMC4616219/

Hassert, D.L., T. Miyashita, and C.L. Williams. "The Effects of
Peripheral Vagal Nerve Stimulation at a Memory-Modulating Intensity on
Norepinephrine Output in the Basolateral Amygdala." Behavioral Neuroscience
Vol. 118, Issue 1, Feb. 2004. https://www.ncbi.nlm.nih.gov/pubmed/14979784

Kong, Nathan W., William R. Gibb, and Matthew C. Tate. "Neuroplasticity: Insights from Patients Harboring Gliomas." Neural Plasticity 5 July 2016. https://www.ncbi.nlm.nih.gov/pmc/articles/PMC4949342/

Kox, Matthijs, et al. "Voluntary Activation of the Sympathetic Nervous System and Attenuation of the Innate Immune Response in Humans." Proceedings of the National Academy of Science USA Vol. 111, No. 20, 20 May 2014. https://www.ncbi.nlm.nih.gov/pmc/articles/PMC4034215/

Krugman, Herbert E. and Eugene L. Hartley. "Passive Learning from Television." Mindful Wellness. http://www.mindfulwellness.us/uploads/9/1/6/2/91629542/passive_learning_from _television_by_herbert_e._krugman_and_eugene_l._hartley.pdf

Mehling, W.E. et al. "Randomized, Control Trial of Breath Therapy for Patients with Chronic Low-Back Pain." Alternative Therapies in Health and Medicine Vol. 11, Issue 4, Jul-Aug. 2005. https://www.ncbi.nlm.nih.gov/pubmed/16053121

Pavlov, Valentin A. and Kevin J. Tracey. "The Vagus Nerve and the Immunity Reflex – Linking Immunity and Metabolism." National Review of Endocrinology Vol. 8, No. 12, Dec. 2012. https://www.ncbi.nlm.nih.gov/pmc/articles/PMC4082307/

Sasmita, Andrew Octavian, Joshua Kuruvilla, and Anna Pick Kiong Ling. "Harnessing Neuroplasticity: Modern Approaches and Clinical Future." International Journal of Neuroscience Vol.128, Issue 11, 4 May 2018. https://www.tandfonline.com/doi/abs/10.1080/00207454.2018.1466781?journalC ode=ines20

Seppala, Emma. "20 Scientific Reasons to Start Meditating today." Psychology Today 11 Sept. 2013. https://www.psychologytoday.com/us/blog/feeling-it/201309/20-scientific-reasons-start-meditating-today

About the Author

Richard L. Haight is the author of *The Unbound Soul* and *Inspirience: Meditation Unbound*, and he is a master-level instructor of martial, meditation and healing arts. Richard began formal martial arts training at age 12 and moved to Japan the age of 24 to advance his training with masters of the sword, staff, and aiki-jujutsu.

During his 15 years living in Japan, Richard was awarded master's licenses in four samurai arts as well as a traditional healing art called Sotai-ho. Richard is one of the world's foremost experts in the traditional Japanese martial arts.

Through his books, his meditation and martial arts seminar, Richard Haight is helping to ignite a worldwide movement for personal transformation that is free of all constraints and open to anyone of any level. Richard Haight now lives and teaches in southern Oregon, U.S.A.

Receiving the License of Full Mastery from Master Shizen Osaki
Kanagawa, Japan, July 2012.

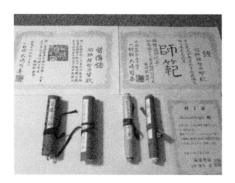

(Top - left to right) License of Full Mastery and Instructors License in Daito-ryu Aikijujutsu
(Mastership Scrolls - left to right) Daito-ryu Aikijujutsu, Yagyu Shinkage-ryu Hyoho,
Shinkage-ryu Jojutsu, Seigo-ryu Battojutsu, Sotai-ho (Master's License)

Front and Center, Shizen Osaki, Sensei
Kanagawa, Japan, October 2017

186

Contact

Here are some ways to connect with Richard Haight's teachings:

- Website: www.richardlhaight.com
- One-Month Free Meditation Class Trial
  www.richardlhaight.com/services
- Publishing Notifications: www.richardlhaight.com/notifications
- YouTube: Tools of Spiritual Awakening with Richard L Haight
- Facebook: www.facebook.com/richardlhaightauthor
- Email: contact@richardlhaight.com

Daily Meditation Training with Richard L Haight

If you would like more hands-on instruction about its meditation and teachings, you can get free 30-day guided meditation training with Richard L Haight.

Visit: www.richardlhaight.com/services

The Unbound Soul

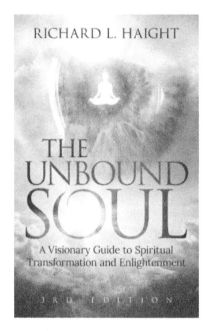

"One of the best Consciousness books of all time"
—BookAuthority

2019 Gold Winner of the Reader's Favorite Awards and bestseller in multiple spirituality, meditation, self-help categories, *The Unbound Soul* is a fresh, highly acclaimed spiritual guide that tells of one man's struggle to free his soul while guiding the reader to their own inner freedom.

The Unbound Soul is a memoir that tells the true story of a young boy, who in the midst of a vision, dedicates his life to spiritual awakening. As he matures, this promise leads him across the globe, gathering ancient knowledge and mastering martial, healing, and meditation arts.

But *The Unbound Soul* is so much more than a memoir. It is a powerful guide that reveals the profoundly simple yet elusive truth that illuminates your life and provides a set of powerful awareness tools to assist you on your personal path. *The Unbound Soul* is really about you and your path toward practical realization in everyday life.

Inspirience

INSPIRIENCE
MEDITATION UNBOUND

THE UNCONDITIONED PATH TO
SPIRITUAL AWAKENING

RICHARD L. HAIGHT

"I read one spiritual book a week for my radio show, and I will tell you that Inspirience is fresh, genuine, and much needed!"
—Jean Adrienne, *PowerTalk Radio*

EXPERIENCING LIFE
INSPIRING CHANGE
LIVING INSPIRIENCE

What is it you truly seek? The reality is, most of us don't really know. Upon close investigation, we discover, above all else, we are seeking the transcendent, that which resides at the deepest place within us, that which connects us to all that is and gives unconditioned meaning to our lives.

The transcendent exceeds the grasp of the mind and the limits of words, for it is beyond all form and definition. But inspirience, although it cannot be explained in words, can be found. There is a path to it.

Richard L. Haight, the bestselling author of *The Unbound Soul*, master meditator and swordsman, shares a simple and natural way to inspirience through unconditioned meditation. *Inspirience* will take you on a journey to the transcendent, so that it can transform your life — *and the world.*

The Psychedelic Path

*"Fascinating insights into visionary states.
Bound to be a controversial book."*
— Grady Harp, *Amazon Hall of Fame Reviewer*

Are you walking the spiritual path and curious about psychedelics? Journey along with a meditation master and former "pharmacological purist" as he explores the spiritual heart of the psychedelic experience to discover the potential benefits and dangers of these substances.

Richard L. Haight, a master swordsman, meditation expert, and bestselling author of *The Unbound Soul* provides an extraordinarily powerful, unbiased account of hallucinogens as they relate to the spiritual path.

For his journeys, Haight makes use of three ancient shamanic plants found in South, Central, and North America, and he reveals a cutting-edge perspective that catalyzes tremendous personal transformation.

Printed in Great Britain
by Amazon